MINDFULNESS SKILLS WORKBOOK FOR CLINICIANS AND CLIENTS

111 Tools, Techniques, Activities & Worksheets

by

Debra E Burdick, LCSWR, BCN

deb@TheBrainLady.com

"Debra Burdick has written a gem of a book on mindfulness. As a guide for clinicians, the book has everything: no-nonsense, clear style; plenty of background info; tie-ins with research; excellent illustrations; and plenty of original experiential tools for introducing mindfulness and leveraging motivation and compliance. This is the kind of resource on mindfulness that you are not just going to skim through: you are going to copy and dog-ear and share this book with your colleagues and your clients. This just might be the last guide to teaching mindfulness that you buy."

Pavel Somov, Ph.D., author of *Present Perfect, Reinventing the Meal and Anger Management Jumpstart*

"Debra's work has changed my life, as well as lives of my patients. As a board certified sleep specialist and neurologist, I began to struggle when I had patients with stress induced symptoms. Initially coming out of medical school, I tried to help with what I was taught to use which is medications. It was very rewarding when it worked. But it was disheartening when it didn't, and even more disappointing when the patient would come back a few times and complain that all I do is increase or change medications.

Like many other physicians, I don't live in an academic university setting and there is a scarcity in the number of psychologist and counselors for the population of stress induced symptoms that we see. I started a quest to see how I can help my patients. I spent a year reading and learning about Mindfulness techniques and Neurobiology. It was enlightening to me, but I still struggled to help my patients. And then I took a full day webinar on the Mindfulness took kit by Deb The Brain Lady. Within a month I was changing lives. I became more efficient in helping my clients achieve sleep, treat pain, and reduce stress.

After conducting her techniques with my clients, I would say 90% of them would comment they felt more relaxed. The other 10% would say they felt different, but didn't know how they felt. I am convinced that these were high stressed clients that had forgotten how it is to feel relaxed, because when I would them directly ask them if they felt relaxed it is as a light bulb came up and they would say "yes".

The Brain Lady's Mindfulness Skills Work Book will allow one to learn the basics of Mindfulness for an introduction, as well as target specific symptoms and challenges the patients are having. I encourage every clinician who wants to change lives to make yourself familiar with the work."

Jose Colon, M.D., M.P.H.

Copyright © 2013 by Debra E Burdick
Published by
PESI Publishing and Media
CMI Education Institute, Inc
3839 White Ave
Eau Claire, WI 54703

Cover Design: Amy Rubenzer
Layout Design: Bookmasters
Edited By: Marietta Whittlesey & Bookmasters

Printed in the United States of America

ISBN: 978-1-93612-845-7

PESI
Publishing
& Media
www.PESI.com

Table of Contents

Section III   Tools for Teaching Specific Mindfulness Skills

Section IV   Tools for Using Mindfulness Skills for Specific Disorders

Section V Tools for Tracking Progress

Appendix

Section I

INTRODUCTION

Chapter 1: Introduction

WHY THIS BOOK IS NEEDED

Mindfulness Toolkit Workbook is specifically designed to meet the needs of mental health practitioners, teachers, and other helping professionals who want to incorporate mindfulness skills into their work. It provides over 100 specific tools that can be used with clients and students to help them experience mindfulness, incorporate it into their daily lives, and reap its proven benefits.

The workbook provides specific tools for:

- Explaining What Mindfulness Is
- Increasing Use of Mindfulness at Home
- Teaching the Basics of Mindfulness
- Teaching a Wide Variety of Specific Mindfulness Skills
- Using Mindfulness Skills for Specific Mental Health Disorders
- Tracking Progress

The workbook explains the theory behind each tool, leads you through the step-by-step process to implement the tool, and then gives you expert guidance on processing the result. It includes tools to explain the neurobiology behind mindfulness in a way your clients can relate to. The workbook also includes a full set of handouts you can use with your clients containing the text of dozens of specific mindfulness skills and meditations. It gives you everything you need to incorporate mindfulness into your practice in a hands-on, practical way that has been proven to be highly effective.

WHAT'S DIFFERENT ABOUT THIS BOOK?

There are many excellent books about mindfulness available today. Most of them provide the theory and research and some examples of mindfulness skills. This *Mindfulness Toolkit Workbook* differs from these other books in that it starts where the others leave off. It contains a practical one-of-a-kind toolkit of effective mindfulness skills that research has proven help people of all ages to improve their mental, physical, and spiritual health. The toolkit consists of step-by-step, easy-to-use tools, techniques, and skills you can use to teach mindfulness to your clients or students and improve treatment outcomes.

HOW TO USE THIS BOOK

The tools provided in this book are organized to provide you with the theory behind each tool, instructions for implementation, and guidelines for processing the result. Step-by-step instructions are provided to help you use the tools with your clients or students. The tools are organized in a logical progression but are designed to be used independently and in any order that makes sense for each particular client.

There are a variety of tools included that call for clients to answer prompts in their journal. Therefore, it is highly recommended that you ask clients to either buy a simple journal or set up a document on their computer in which they can write as they learn and practice the mindfulness skills presented in this book.

For convenience the tools described in this book will reference their use with "clients." Please translate the word "client" to whatever term you use for the people you work with, such as "patient" or "student" or "yourself." Thank you.

Section II

TOOLS FOR INTEGRATING MINDFULNESS IN PRACTICE

Chapter 2: Tools for Explaining Mindfulness

DEFINING MINDFULNESS

Tool 2-1: Define Mindfulness

THEORY: Many clients have no real concept of what mindfulness is or how it could help them. Therefore, it is important to use a simple, basic definition to introduce the concept. As clients use more of the tools in this workbook, they will develop their own personal understanding of what mindfulness means to them. Caution: Some clients are totally put off by the word "meditation," picturing a process of sitting completely still with no thoughts for 20 or 30 minutes. This is a totally overwhelming and unbearable concept for many, particularly if they have ADHD or experience anxiety. Most of the mindfulness tools included here teach the process of gradually becoming better at dismissing distracting thoughts and gaining the ability to "meditate." But start small, where the client is, so you don't turn them off to the process. Most of the mindfulness skills do not require sitting still for long. This tool introduces Jon Kabat-Zinn's (Kabat-Zinn, 2003) definition of mindfulness.

IMPLEMENTATION: Use the simple definition in Handout 2-1 to explain what mindfulness is. Then break it down and go over each component of the definition. For example, start with "paying attention to something." This can be anything you choose to pay attention to. It often begins with paying attention to the breath but it could also be paying attention to your surroundings, driving, eating, washing the dishes, your thoughts or emotions, taking a shower, your physical body, or even your children. Then go over "in a particular way" and discuss what that means, such as focusing your attention, closing your eyes and going within, looking at something, listening, tasting, smelling, or touching. Next, discuss "on purpose," which simply means that you set the intention and decide to pay attention to this specific "something." "In the present moment" means right now, while dismissing thoughts of the past or future that arise in the present. "Non-judgmentally" means without assessing. It means not to compare, judge, or be critical of yourself or what arises while paying attention.

PROCESS: Initiate a discussion with your client about their reaction to hearing this definition. Ask them to think of examples of how they might do each part of the definition. For example, ask them to choose something to pay attention to. Ask them how they will focus on it (visual, auditory, tactile senses, etc.). Discuss how once they've set the intention to focus on something, they can then focus "on purpose." Ask how they would stay in the present moment. Discuss judgment and how commonly we all do it, and what it feels like not to judge. Ask them to write their own definition of Mindfulness in words that resonate with them.

Mindfulness

Paying attention to
something,
in a particular way,
on purpose,
in the present moment,
non-judgmentally.

(Kabat-Zinn, 2003)

Tool 2-2: Illustrate Mindfulness Concept with Snow Globe or Water with Baking Soda

THEORY: With 60,000 thoughts a day (and the emotions they evoke) whirling through the mind, it is easy to understand how the mind can get cluttered, overwhelmed, and unfocused. A calm, clear mind can be easily overwhelmed by the constant flow of thoughts, feelings, and sensations. This exercise illustrates the concept of mindfulness as clarity of mind, clearing away the clutter, settling down, calming. It provides a great way to visualize mindfulness.

IMPLEMENTATION: Explain that this exercise will give clients a way to visualize their mind calming down. Do the Cloudy Versus Clear Mind exercise described in Handout 2-2.

PROCESSING: Ask the client how they felt as they watched the baking soda swirling around and making the water murky. Ask them what they noticed as they watched the water clear. Were they able to calm their mind as the water cleared? Did they feel more calm in their body? Could they relate to the comparison of cloudy versus clear water to a cloudy versus clear mind?

HANDOUT 2-2
CLOUDY VERSUS CLEAR MIND

Place clear water in a glass bowl.

Place some colorful rocks or shells or small objects around the outside of the bowl.

Ask the client to look through the bowl to the other side of the room and/or at the objects around the outside of the bowl.

Then sprinkle some baking soda into the water and watch the water get cloudy and the objects around the bowl disappear.

Explain that this is what happens in their mind when they are worried, angry, distracted, stressed out, or revved up, and their thoughts and feelings are whirling around.

Guide them to keep watching the water in the bowl to see what happens as the baking soda settles to the bottom.

Tell them that's what mindful breathing does for their mind. It clears and calms their mind, settles their thoughts and feelings, and helps them to feel more relaxed and better able to concentrate.

Then tell them to wiggle their body to get their mind revved up again while stirring the water or adding more baking soda.

Show them how cloudy the water is again—like their mind—and watch it settle as they sit quietly breathing and watching. Ask them to raise their hand when they can see through the water again.

Tell them to breathe slowly as they watch the water clear. Explain that by breathing slowly and steadily their thoughts and feelings settle and their minds become clear.

Another way to do this is with a snow globe or glitter ball. Just shake the globe or ball and follow the same process described here.

Tool 2-3: Compare Mindfulness to the Rest in Music

THEORY: Mindfulness can be thought of like a rest in music. The rest in music is a place where the music stops for a brief moment, in time with the overall rhythm of the song. It is an interval of silence. The rest is just as important to the song as the sounds. It informs the music like mindfulness informs life. Mindfulness can be thought of as a rest from the busy activity of the mind. It puts a brief pause in the chatter. It improves mental clarity.

IMPLEMENTATION: Explain that a rest in music is a brief interval of silence where the music or melody stops for a moment. Choose some music that is appropriate for the age and interests of the client. Ask them to listen and raise their hand each time they hear a rest in the music or in any particular instrument.

Another way to do this is to ask the client to clap four times in a row with an even beat and count one, two, three, four, as they clap. Now ask them to clap two times, hold one beat, and clap on beat four—clap, clap, hold, clap. Play with it. Change the pattern—clap, hold, clap, clap. Hold two beats instead of one—clap, hold, hold, clap. Change the beat to one, two, three.

PROCESSING: Were they able to notice the rests in the music? How would the music change without the rest? Discuss what a rest might look like in their life. What would a rest improve in their life?

CORE SKILLS

Tool 2-4: Set Intention

THEORY:　Setting intention is a basic step in any practice. Intention is the goal you wish to achieve from an action. It is your directed attention. In mindfulness, intention refers to what you are choosing to pay attention to. Your intention might be to pay attention to your breath. It might be to pay attention to the task at hand or to your surroundings. Being mindful involves bringing your attention back to your intention over and over again. This tool explains the process of setting intention at the beginning of mindfulness practice.

Implementation:

- Decide what your intention is.
    - Identify your intention at the beginning of every mindfulness practice whether formal or not. For example, if you intend to do an Awareness of Breath Meditation (Tool 5-5), set your intention to focus your attention on your breath.
- Keep awareness of your intention present in mind.
    - Remind yourself as soon as you become aware of a thought, feeling, or distraction that your intention is to focus on your breath, and shift your attention back to your breath.
- Check in periodically to ensure your thoughts, words, and actions remain consistent with your intention.
- Do this over and over during the entire Awareness of Breath or any mindfulness practice.

Being mindful while doing a task is an example of a less formal mindfulness practice. Set your intention to be mindful while doing whatever task you choose. If you are practicing mindfulness when eating, then set your intention to focus your attention on the entire process of eating. Read the "Awareness of Eating" exercise on Handout 2-4 to your client. Reflect on their experience with them. Encourage them to practice mindful eating whenever they eat. Remind them that setting intention is the first step in practicing any mindfulness skill.

See Tool 13-1 for a structured method for clarifying intention.

PROCESSING:　Help clients reflect on what it was like for them to set an intention. Ask them: How difficult or easy was it to set your intention? Did you find your mind wandering from your intention? How did you bring it back to your intention? What did you notice when you listened to the Awareness of Eating exercise? How can you apply this process of setting intention to your daily life? Ask them to practice awareness of eating whenever they eat and discuss what happens when they do so.

HANDOUT 2-4
MINDFULNESS OF INTENTION PRACTICE: AWARENESS OF EATING

Set your intention to focus your full attention on the process of eating. Whenever other thoughts arise, notice them, dismiss them, and remind yourself of your intention to pay attention to eating. Notice how the food looks as it sits on your plate. Be aware of the food's aroma, color, shape. Before you start to eat, notice how your stomach feels. Does it feel hungry, empty? Is it comfortable, uncomfortable? Can you connect how it feels with hunger? Tune in to how your stomach feels and make sure you are hungry before you eat.

As you put the food on your fork, notice its weight and consistency. As you place the food in your mouth, notice the aroma, the temperature, how it feels in your mouth. As you chew, focus on the flavor, the texture, the chewiness. Pay attention to how it feels when you chew the food. Notice if it is tender, tough, slippery, smooth, rough, tangy, sweet, sour, hot, or cold. Be aware of whether it sticks to your teeth. If your mind wanders, just remember your intention and bring your attention back to eating. Again notice the feeling of the food in your mouth, on your teeth, on your tongue, on your lips. Chew until it is completely ready to be swallowed. Pay attention to how the food feels as you swallow and it leaves your mouth and slides down your throat. Notice if there is any food still in your mouth or if it's empty now. Tune in to how your stomach feels. Notice how it feels different after you have eaten a little food and then after you have eaten a lot of food. Repeat this process until your food is gone or until you feel full.

Tool 2-5: Cultivate a Witnessing Awareness

THEORY: Being "aware of awareness" is a revolutionary idea for many people. The idea is to notice what's arising as it is arising. This includes awareness of thoughts, feelings, body sensations, and physical surroundings. It involves paying attention to what is happening in this moment and acknowledging and dismissing distractions. The goal is to remain aware without trying to change anything. Observe and accept what you observe. Awareness is the first step in eventually being able to change unwanted patterns.

IMPLEMENTATION: Guide clients in the following process.

> Stop. Pause for a moment.
>
> Notice what's arising as it's arising.
>
> Pay attention to thoughts, feelings, body sensations, surroundings.
>
> Just be aware without trying to change anything.
>
> As distractions occur, remember your intention and bring your attention back to what's arising.
>
> Continue for 30 seconds, increasing gradually to 5 minutes.

PROCESSING: Help clients reflect on what their experience was like when doing this mindfulness exercise. Ask them: What did you notice? What thoughts arose? Were you aware of any feelings? Were body sensations a part of your awareness? What distracted you? How did you refocus on being a witness to your awareness?

Tool 2-6: Regulate Attention

THEORY: We live in a very distracting and distracted culture. We often feel overwhelmed and overloaded with many things competing for our attention. Being able to regulate our attention improves concentration, memory, and overall mental clarity. This tool provides the basic steps involved in improving the ability to regulate attention and to pay attention on purpose.

IMPLEMENTATION: Lead clients in the following meditation after helping them decide what they intend to pay attention to.

> Set your intention to pay attention.
>
> Select something to pay attention to. This might be your breath, or the feeling of your hands as you rub them together, or any object in your surroundings or outside in nature such as the leaves on a tree.
>
> Now just notice everything you can about the object of your attention.
>
> Notice if you are being distracted by a thought, feeling, body sensation, or something in your environment.
>
> Acknowledge the distraction and dismiss it without judging.
>
> Just let it go.
>
> Return your focus to the intended object of your attention.
>
> Notice the details of whatever you have chosen to focus on.
>
> Notice how it looks, how it feels, how it smells.
>
> Continue this process in silence for 1 minute.

As you practice this, gradually increase the time by 1 minute each time until you are doing it for 5 minutes or up to 15 minutes for more advanced practice.

PROCESSING: Explore what the client experienced. Ask them: Did your mind wander as you did this exercise? What did you do when you noticed you were distracted? What did you notice about the object of your attention? Have you ever noticed this before? Were you aware of any inner dialogue commenting on the process?

Tool 2-7: Strengthen Self-Regulation—Use a Word or Color as Body–Mind Signal

THEORY: Practicing mindfulness increases the brain's ability to regulate itself. Neuronal pathways are created and strengthened by the repeated practice of calming the mind and paying attention to something on purpose. Mindfulness can decrease the emotional hijacking that occurs often below the level of awareness.

IMPLEMENTATION: Explain that repeating a word or picturing a color often helps one stay focused. Ask clients to choose a word or a color to use to help them stay focused.

Tell clients: For example you might repeat "driving, driving" when driving a car to remind yourself to be mindful and pay attention to driving while driving. Or you might silently repeat "breathing, breathing" during a breathing meditation or when you need a brief break. You might use the words "mindful, mindful" to remind yourself to stay in the present and be aware of whatever task or practice you are doing at the moment.

Some people find that picturing a color of their choosing helps them stay focused better than using a word. Choose a color that is significant or pleasing to you. For example, you might picture the color blue whenever you feel stressed to remind yourself to breathe so you can lower your stress response. Or you might picture yellow to remind yourself to be mindful while performing the task at hand. Experiment with different colors until you find the best one(s) for you.

PROCESSING: Explore what works best with clients by asking: What words work best for you? Do you prefer to use a color? What color did you choose? How did you use this skill during the past week? How might you have used it? Did you notice any improvement in your ability to regulate your thoughts or feelings?

Tool 2-8: Loving Kindness for Self and Others

THEORY: Negative self-talk starts very young. Unfortunately, children often receive a lot of negative messages about themselves. One 6-year-old boy with hyperactivity associated with ADHD told me he knew his new medicine was working because "no one yelled at me all day." The negative messages may come from parents, teachers, peers, and often the media. This sets up competitiveness and a pattern of self-judgment. Many people experience trauma and core wounds as they journey through life. Studies show that Loving Kindness exercises foster acceptance and compassion for self and others (Hutcherson, Seppala, & Gross, 2008; Kabat-Zinn, 1990; The Dalai Lama, 2001).

IMPLEMENTATION: Explain to clients that the practice of loving kindness feels good and helps them develop acceptance and compassion for themselves and others. Teach them that the practice of loving kindness always begins with developing a loving acceptance of yourself. Then you are ready to systematically develop loving kindness toward others.

Use Handout 2-8 to explain the loving kindness mindfulness exercise. Explain that there are five types of persons to develop loving kindness toward:

- Yourself
- A good friend
- A "neutral" person
- A difficult person
- All four of the above equally
- And then gradually the entire universe

Guide clients to picture each of these people in their mind and send them loving kindness each in turn as described in the handout.

PROCESSING: Process what this exercise was like with your clients. Ask them: Did you have difficulty sending loving kindness to yourself? Did you feel any different when sending loving kindness to a friend versus a difficult person? What did you notice about your attitude before, during, and after the exercise?

HANDOUT 2-8
LOVING KINDNESS FOR SELF AND OTHERS

Five types of persons to develop loving-kindness toward:

• Yourself
• A good friend
• A "neutral" person
• A difficult person
• All four of the above equally
• And then gradually the entire universe

Picture each of these people in your mind and send them loving kindness each in turn such as:

> May I be well.
> May I be happy.
> May I be free from suffering.
> May my good friend be well.
> May my good friend be happy.
> May my good friend be free from suffering.
> May the neutral person I am picturing be well.
> May the neutral person I am picturing be happy.
> May the neutral person I am picturing be free from suffering.
> May this person I find difficult be well.
> May this person I find difficult be happy.
> May this person I find difficult be free from suffering.
> May all of these people including me be well.
> May all of these people including me be happy.
> May all of these people including me be free from suffering.
> May the entire universe be well.
> May the entire universe be happy.
> May the entire universe be free from suffering.

Or

> May I live in safety.
> May I have mental happiness (peace or joy).
> May I have physical happiness (health).
> May I live with ease.
> May my good friend live in safety.
> May my good friend have mental happiness (peace or joy).
> May my good friend have physical happiness (health).
> May my good friend live with ease.
> *[continue with each type of person]*

Or

> I know I (they) suffer.
> Inhale the dark cloud that's around me (them).
> Transform and generate the white light of compassion.
> Exhale slowly three times.
> *[continue with each type of person]*

Tool 2-9: Journal About Your Understanding of What Mindfulness is

THEORY: Journaling can be an effective way for clients to process and integrate their experiences while learning mindfulness. Some clients will love to journal. Others will not. If a client is not comfortable writing, ask them to draw a picture that represents something about their experience with a basic mindfulness skill such as awareness of breathing. If they don't want to journal, you might still ask them the following prompts and process their verbal responses. Ask them to buy a nicely covered blank journal or else set up a document on their computer, whichever will be most convenient for them.

IMPLEMENTATION: No matter whether you are a mindfulness novice or an experienced mindfulness practitioner, journaling can help you process and integrate how mindfulness is affecting your life. Instruct clients to answer the journal prompts on Handout 2-9.

PROCESSING: Ask your client if they have done the journaling and if they would feel comfortable sharing what they wrote. Explore their answers. Help them clarify their intention. Discuss the process from wherever they are starting mindfulness practice.

JOURNAL ABOUT YOUR UNDERSTANDING OF WHAT MINDFULNESS IS

Journal Prompts:

- How would you define mindfulness?
- How does your new understanding about mindfulness differ from what you thought it was?
- Why have you decided to incorporate mindfulness in your life?
- Thus far, what have you noticed about yourself while practicing the core skills?
- How have you started to be more mindful during your day?
- What do you hope to change or improve by being more mindful?
- What is your intention for mindfulness practice?
- Write about the core skills of mindfulness and how they interrelate.
- How do you feel about being more mindful?

THE NEUROBIOLOGY OF WHY MINDFULNESS WORKS
TOOLS FOR EXPLAINING NEUROPLASTICITY

Tool 2-10: What is Neuroplasticity and Why Do We Care?

THEORY:　Neuroplasticity is the ability of the brain to change itself. MRI studies, SPECT scan studies, and EEG studies confirm the ability of mindfulness practice to change brain structure as well as brain functioning. Studies show improvements in self-regulation, mood, well-being, self-esteem, concentration, sleep, health, addictions, memory and so much more. (See Handout 2-20 for research references.) Therefore, mindfulness practice is an excellent way to trigger positive neuroplastic changes in the brain.

IMPLEMENTATION:　Explain that the brain's ability to change itself is called neuroplasticity. Use the two exercises (Paths in the Grass and Paper Folding) in Handout 2-10 to illustrate how neuronal pathways are "worn" into the brain. Discuss how this may be helpful, such as when we learn something new, or harmful if the brain gets stuck in a negative pattern such as anxiety or depression. Use the handout to explore how doing something a different way starts to change the pathway, which can be very helpful when shifting out of negative mood states or anxious tendencies.

PROCESSING:　Help clients explore how the process of neuroplasticity may be helping them or keeping them stuck by asking: What positive or negative things do you do repeatedly that may have worn a "pathway" in your brain? Do you notice yourself responding automatically to things without stopping to think and choosing a response? Are there any pathways you would like to reinforce or eliminate? Does fear or anxiety play a role in your life? In what ways do you feel stuck?

HANDOUT 2-10-1
WHAT IS NEUROPLASTICITY AND WHY DO WE CARE?

PATHS IN THE GRASS

Close your eyes and picture a lawn of green grass.

Now imagine that someone walks across the grass diagonally from one corner of the lawn to the opposite corner.

Notice how the grass changes. Perhaps the grass is a bit matted down where they walked.

Now imagine lots of people walking across the grass following the same path.
After a while, notice that some of the grass is dying where so many footsteps have fallen.

Imagine that this process continues until there is a path worn in the lawn where there is no longer any grass—just a dirt path worn smooth from all the foot traffic.

This is like the process of neuroplasticity in the brain. According to Hebb's axiom, neurons that fire together wire together (Hebb, 2009), and dendrites increase in size and efficiency when something is repeated over and over. So, like the path worn in the grass, the neuronal pathway gets stronger and stronger with repetition. Mindfulness practice is an effective way to create more healthy "pathways" in the brain.

Now imagine the lawn with the path across it. Notice what happens to it over time when no one walks on it anymore. The grass slowly starts to grow where the path was until at some point there is no longer a path at all. Mindfulness practice can help rewire the brain so it no longer automatically responds with anxiety, or anger, or fear, or feeling stressed. Mindfulness helps to decrease the negative pathways in the brain.

- Ask clients to fold a piece of paper, then fold it again, and then again.
- Have them unfold it and fold it again where it was already folded.
- Ask them if refolding is faster and easier than folding in the first place.
- Relate this to moving information along a well-traveled path of neurons.
- Discuss whether it is easier for your brain to think something new or the same thought.
- Ask them if it is easier to learn something new or do something you have done before.

TOOLS FOR EXPLAINING IMPLICIT MEMORY

Tool 2-11: How to Describe Implicit Memory

THEORY: Implicit memory is encoded throughout our lives starting at birth (some believe it starts in the womb). Dan Siegel states that it involves perception, emotion, bodily sensation, behavior, mental models, and priming (Siegel, 2010). Essentially, implicit memory is a memory that you don't realize you are retrieving from the past. Implicit memory is useful and necessary as it involves recollection of skills and things you know how to do that you don't need to recall consciously. For example, implicit memory helps you remember how to ride a bike without consciously feeling like you are having a memory of learning to ride. Implicit memory starts below the level of awareness and drives current behavior.

Implicit memory can be particularly troublesome in the present if you experienced intense emotions or trauma in the past. The implicit memory of these things can emotionally hijack you in the present without your being aware this is happening. This is where mindfulness practice can be helpful to increase awareness.

IMPLEMENTATION: Use the following information to explain what implicit memory is and why it's important to use mindfulness to prevent implicit memory from driving behavior in negative ways.

What is implicit memory?

- Encoded throughout our lives.
- Probably the only type of memory infants have.
- Allows us to remember how to do something without being conscious of how to do it, such as riding a bicycle, walking—anything procedural.
- Gets stored without our conscious awareness.
- Gets retrieved without our awareness—"I don't know I'm having a memory."
- Past memories come flooding in without knowing they're from the past; it feels like it is all coming from the present.
- Drives behavior without our awareness—often negatively.
- Primes us to respond in a certain fashion.
- Readies us for the future.
- Designed to protect us.
- Can create here and now perceptions and beliefs that are actually from the past.
- Can show up as a physical feeling in our body, an emotional reaction, a behavioral pattern, or a bias.
- The amygdala is responsible for implicit memory as it scans earlier memories of danger.
- Procedural memory is a subset (how to do things).

Why do we care?

- Implicit memories can emotionally hijack our prefrontal cortex and drive behavior without our awareness.
- Can often create a total misinterpretation of a current situation.

- Implicit memory is like the child that lives within us.
- Implicit memories may show up in body sensations.
- Mindfulness allows us to integrate implicit with explicit memory to improve emotional response and behavioral patterns.

Examples of implicit memory in action:

- Riding a bicycle, walking, speaking, driving a car.
- Your parents yelled at you when you didn't understand your math homework and now you hate math but don't realize why.
- No one picked you for their team in elementary school to play basketball and after that you never really enjoyed sports.
- Your father was always putting you down and now you never feel you are good enough but you don't know why.
- A beloved boyfriend cheated on you when you were a teenager and now you distrust all men.
- You fell off your bicycle the first time you tried to learn to ride and broke your arm. Now you are afraid you will fail if you try something new.
- You had a car crash and dealt with it calmly and without emotion. A few months later your car hits a curb and you burst out crying without knowing why. When you explore it, you realize the car made the same sound when it hit the curb as it did during the car crash. You could consciously remember the details of the car crash (explicit memory) but not the emotion triggered by the crash sound (implicit memory).

Exercise

- Make a list of implicit memories that are procedural in nature.
- Make a list of things that might happen to a person that could drive behavior beneath their awareness.
- Make a list of issues that tend to recur in your life that might be coming from past experiences.
- Identify an implicit memory that you have become aware of.

PROCESSING: The goal of this tool is to help the client understand what implicit memory is and how it may be operating in their own life. Use this information to help them if they are stuck, have an irrational belief, or a behavior pattern that doesn't serve them. Ask them to tell you about the problem they are experiencing. Then lead them in a Body Scan (Tool 9-1) and see if anything shows up in their body that they can relate to a past memory. Help them integrate the implicit memory with an explicit memory by asking about the details of what was going on when that implicit memory may have been stored. An example might be, if they tell you their childhood was "normal," to ask them to remember and describe some specific details of their family life or a specific interaction with one of their parents (an explicit memory). This may trigger an associated implicit memory.

Tool 2-12: Journal About a Favorite Memory (Explicit Memory)

THEORY: Explicit memory is a memory you know you are having. It emerges by the time a child is about 2 years old. There are two kinds of explicit memories: factual and episodic. The hippocampus (dual and located in the limbic system) encodes explicit memory and enables us to know about the world and ourselves. The hippocampus often shuts down when intense emotions are experienced and prevents explicit memories from being stored. If the hippocampus stays on line during an emotional experience, the memory seems to be easier to remember. This tool helps clients understand and explore personal explicit memories.

IMPLEMENTATION: Use the following journal prompts to help clients understand explicit memory.

Journal Prompts:

- List three explicit memories you have from childhood.
- Are they positive or negative?
- Pick one memory and describe it in detail. You might like to draw it.
- What implicit memory might be associated with this explicit memory?
- Are there any feelings that arise when you remember this memory?
- If possible, talk to someone else who was present when you had this experience and see if they remember it the same way you do.

PROCESSING: This exercise helps people improve their ability to increase self-awareness as well as "awareness of awareness." Ask the client to describe a specific memory and then go deeper to help them access the emotional content of the memory that may have been stored as an implicit memory. Discuss how this implicit memory may be activated in the present.

TOOLS FOR EXPLAINING BRAIN STRUCTURE RELEVANT TO MINDFULNESS

Tool 2-13: The Prefrontal Cortex (PFC)

THEORY: The prefrontal cortex (PFC) can be thought of as the conductor of the brain as it orchestrates thoughts and actions according to internal goals. It links the cortex, limbic areas, and brainstem and carries out executive functions. One study showed that mindful breathing practice increased PFC activation, which may reflect stronger processing of distracting events and emotions, respectively (Hölzel et al., 2007b).

IMPLEMENTATION: Explain that the prefrontal cortex is located in the frontal lobe of the brain. It acts like a conductor, controlling the activities of the rest of the brain. It is involved in planning complex cognitive behavior, personality expression, decision making, and moderating social behavior. The executive functions are performed in the PFC. Use Handout 2-13 to explain the functions of the PFC and to compare it to the functions of a conductor of an orchestra.

PROCESSING: Review the location and function of the PFC. Explore some examples of difficulties that occur if the PFC isn't working optimally such as ADHD, depression, stress response, being overwhelmed, disorganization, poor planning, depressed mood, and poor emotional regulation. Relate these to any issues your client may be experiencing.

HANDOUT 2-13
THE PREFRONTAL CORTEX (PFC)

The following executive functions are performed by the PFC:

- Planning
- Organizing
- Regulating Attention
- Decision Making
- Moderating Behavior
- Personality Expression
- Motivation
- Mood

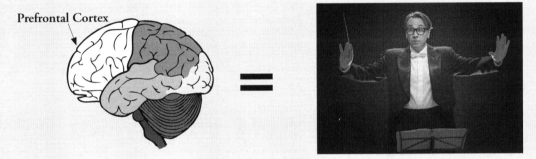

Prefrontal Cortex

EXERCISE

- What does a conductor do in an orchestra?
- Imagine that your PFC is the conductor of your brain. List the ways it "conducts" the activities of your brain, particularly the executive functions.
- List things you have trouble doing that are controlled by the PFC.
- List things you do well that are controlled by the PFC.
- Practice strengthening PFC processing by practicing mindfulness skills.
- What might happen if the PFC is offline and not working well?

Tool 2-14: The Amygdala—Security Guard

THEORY: The amygdala consists of two almond-shaped brain structures that, along with the hippocampus, are part of the limbic system. It plays a key role in the processing of emotions and is central to survival, arousal, and autonomic responses. It is associated with fear responses, hormonal secretions, and emotional (implicit) memory. It is essentially the security guard in our brain and is designed to keep us safe. A 2010 study (Hotzel, Lazar, et al., 2010) shows that reductions in stress (which mindfulness enables) can actually decrease the grey matter density of the amygdala.

IMPLEMENTATION: Explain to clients that the amygdala acts like the security guard, panic button, smoke detector, watch dog, or fear center of the brain. Mindfulness calms the activity of the amygdala and increases a feeling of calm and clarity. Ask clients what a security guard does. Use Handout 2-14 to explore how the amygdala works to keep clients safe and how to calm an over-activated amygdala.

Amygdala

PROCESSING: Help your client explain what the amygdala is and what its function is. Show them the graphic representation of where it is in the brain. Help them explore when their amygdala might have been doing its job. Discuss how to use mindfulness tools, such as awareness of breath and relaxation breathing, to calm the amygdala.

EXERCISE

- List 2 or 3 times when you think your amygdala was activated to keep you safe. Were there any times you were actually safe in the present but your amygdala thought you were in danger based on an implicit memory of something that happened in the past?

- Use the Awareness of Breath (Tool 5-5) and Relaxation Breath (Tool 5-1) tools to calm your amygdala.

- Study the following diagram, which illustrates how information intended for the PFC gets derailed when the amygdala gets activated.

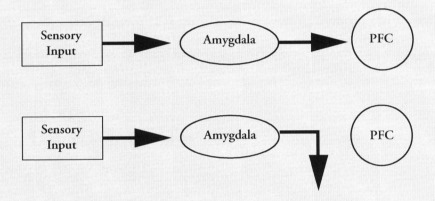

What happens in a Fight, Flight or Freeze Response

Tool 2-15: The Insula

THEORY: Studies show that mindfulness changes the structure of the insula—specifically, the right anterior insula (Hölzel et al., 2007a). Greater right anterior insular gray matter volume correlates with increased accuracy in the subjective sense of the body and with negative emotional experience as well as increased sustained attention. This tool helps clients understand the function of the insula and helps them improve a key core mindfulness skill. Knowing that mindfulness actually changes brain structure in positive ways helps clients understand the benefits and improves the chances they will practice mindfulness.

IMPLEMENTATION: Use Handout 2-15A to review the location and function of the insula. Discuss the research that found increased thickness of the cerebral cortex in the insula in meditators and relate this to improvements in all the functions of the insula. (See Tool 2-20.)

Use the Taking Your Pulse Handout 2-15B to help clients practice taking their pulse, which is a self-awareness mindfulness skill associated with the insula.

The insula is also involved in subjective emotional experience. Use the Awareness of Emotions Tool 8-1 to help them increase awareness of their emotional landscape.

PROCESSING: This tool combines a basic knowledge about how mindfulness changes the brain with two exercises that foster this change. Guide your client on taking their pulse, slowing down and counting it, and exercising a bit to speed it up. Then ask them what they noticed about their pulse in particular and other body sensations in general. Encourage them to take their pulse to monitor their arousal state as they calm themselves in a stressful situation. Use the Awareness of Emotions Tool 8-1 to practice this skill. Process what came up for them during the exercise.

The insula is involved in:

- Interoception (sensing state of gut, heart, pain, etc.)
- Body movement
- Self-recognition
- Vocalization and music
- Emotional awareness
- Risk, uncertainty, and anticipation
- Visual and auditory awareness of movement
- Time perception
- Attention
- Perceptual decision making
- Cognitive control and performance monitoring

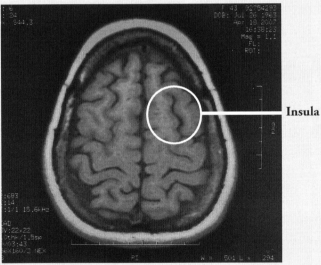

Studies show that meditators:

- have increased thickness of the cerebral cortex in the insula,
- which leads to increased accuracy in the subjective sense of the body and with negative emotional experience,
- as well as increased sustained attention.

Interoception is a function of the insula and includes the awareness of body states. A simple way to understand this concept is to take your pulse.

When our heart beats, we can feel it pumping blood. The way and rate the heart pumps blood is our pulse.

There are two places where we can feel our pulse. First, we can take our first two fingers and place them on our wrist on the palm side of our arm. (Demonstrate this.) If you put your fingers there very gently and don't press down, you may feel as if something is lightly tapping on your fingers. Move your fingers around a little and sit quietly until you can feel it.

The second place is on our neck. Take your first two fingers and place them on the front of your neck below your jaw and above your chest. Gently place them there and move them around until you feel the pulse.

Let's make it easier to feel your pulse. Stand up. Now bend over and touch your toes 10 times fast. Stand up.

Now put your finger lightly on the side of your neck. Can you feel your pulse now? Can you count the beats?

When you are angry, scared, revved up, stressed, or you have been exercising, your heart beats faster and it makes it easier to feel your pulse.

Now sit back down. Breathe in slowly through your nose and gently blow out like you are blowing a huge bubble. Do it again.

Now take your pulse again. Can you feel it? Is it slower? Is it harder to feel?

Now that you know how to take your pulse, you can tell if you need to calm down. You know how to calm down by paying attention to your breathing and taking a slow, deep belly breath and blowing it out slowly.

Tool 2-16: Journal About a Time You Felt Afraid

THEORY: Fear often gets encoded as an implicit memory. Making these implicit memories more conscious can help to integrate them with explicit memories, which can decrease their power over life in the present. Journaling is an excellent way to get in touch with these implicit memories and the associated feelings.

IMPLEMENTATION: Implicit memories are often associated with fear and trauma. After using the previous tools to explain implicit and explicit memory, give Handout 2-16, which contains journal prompts, to clients to help them increase awareness of how implicit memories may be operating in their life.

PROCESSING: Ask your client if they want to share their journal entries with you. Either way, explore their feelings about doing the journal entry and, if possible, process their answers. Help them sort out rational versus irrational fear or fear that is based in the present versus based on a past experience. Relate the fear response to the function of the amygdala.

HANDOUT 2-16
JOURNAL ABOUT A TIME YOU FELT AFRAID

Journal Prompts:

- List some times in your life when you felt afraid.
- Describe what was going on at that time that caused your fear.
- Was there a cause for the fear when you experienced it or was it based on a past experience?
- Was there another time in the past that you experienced that same fear?
- How did you know you were afraid?
- Did you experience a physical sensation in your body when you were afraid?
- What happened to your ability to think and problem-solve when you were afraid?
- Is there anything that used to frighten you that doesn't anymore?
- What are you most afraid of right now?
- What skills do you use to calm yourself down and decrease your fear response?
- How does feeling afraid differ from when you feel stressed, or does it?

TOOLS FOR EASY WAYS TO ENVISION BRAIN ANATOMY

Tool 2-17: Hand Model of the Brain

THEORY: Using a hand model of the brain can help people visualize and understand the structure and function of the brain. There are two helpful options for using the hands as a model for brain structure: a two-fisted model and a model described by Dan Siegel in his book *Mindsight* (Siegel, 2010).

IMPLEMENTATION: Use Handouts 2-17A and 2-17B containing hand models for understanding the brain to give clients a "handy" way to conceptualize the areas of the brain. Show them the different areas of the brain using each model using their own hands.

PROCESSING: Ask the client to practice describing the basic structure of the brain by using each of the hand models. You might suggest they use Siegel's hand model of the brain to illustrate what happens when they get upset, angry, afraid, or stressed by having them raise their fingers to simulate "flipping their lid." Then have them lower their fingers to simulate the prefrontal cortex regaining control of their limbic system and emotions.

HANDOUT 2-17A
SIEGEL'S HAND MODEL OF THE BRAIN

Dan Siegel's hand model of the brain:

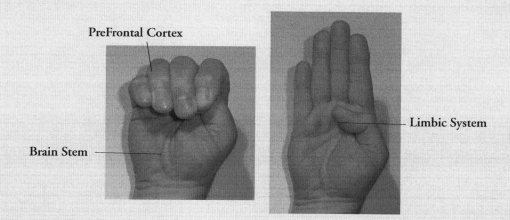

- Hold up each hand with the thumb in the middle of the palm and the fingers curled over the top of the thumb.
- The face is in the front of the knuckles and the back of the head is toward the back of the hand.
- The wrist represents the spinal cord and the base of the hand the brain stem.
- The thumb represents the location of the limbic system.
- The ends of the fingers (from the fingernails to first knuckle) represent the prefrontal cortex.
- The second knuckle represents the cerebral cortex.
- The third knuckle represents the parietal lobes where sensory integration occurs.
- The fingers curled over the thumb illustrate how the prefrontal cortex communicates with most of the brain and particularly helps to control the limbic system. Siegel explains that when we are angry or stressed, the prefrontal cortex loses control of the limbic system, which he illustrates by raising the fingers up straight. He calls this "flipping your lid."

HANDOUT 2-17B
TWO-FISTED MODEL OF THE BRAIN

This brain model uses two closed fists facing each other with thumbs facing you.

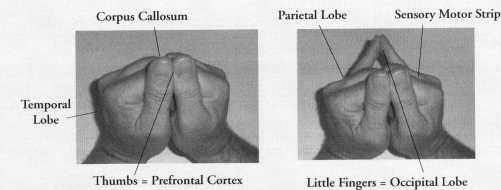

Corpus Callosum

Temporal Lobe

Thumbs = Prefrontal Cortex

Parietal Lobe

Sensory Motor Strip

Little Fingers = Occipital Lobe

- Make each hand into a fist. Hold the fists next to each other with fingernails touching and the thumbs facing you. The thumbs represent the frontal lobe of the brain. This is where the conductor for your brain is located, the area where wise decisions are made. This is also associated with paying attention, reasoning, planning, emotions, and problem solving.
- Lift the little fingers up. These represent the occipital lobe where visual processing takes place.
- Where the knuckles touch represents the corpus callosum, the large nerve fiber connecting the right and left sides of the brain, which allows information to be transferred between the lobes.
- The top of the ring fingers represents the parietal lobes of the brain where sensory processing occurs—touch, sound—and where body perception occurs.
- From one side to the other between the middle and ring fingers represents the sensory motor strip, which divides the front motor cortex from the back sensory cortex.
- Move the hands up beside your head and cup your ears. The knuckles are the outside of the brain model and correspond to the temporal lobes where the amygdala and hippocampus reside. The temporal lobes process auditory information, memory, emotional responses, and visual perception.

Tool 2-18: Neurons—Hand-to-Elbow Model

THEORY: Information in the brain (electrochemical signals) flows across neurons from the dendrites along the axon out to nerve endings, and across the synapse to the next dendrite. This tool gives the client a basic, concrete way to understand how information flows across the neurons and from neuron to neuron.

IMPLEMENTATION:

- Review Handout 2-18 with your client. Explain the flow of information from the dendrites (hand) along the axon (arm) out the nerve ending (elbow) across the synapse (gap) to the next dendrite (hand). Ask the client to use their hand and arm to show the different parts of the neuron.

- Ask clients to pass a coin to each other (or to you, if they are alone) as described in the handout. Ask them what happens as they pass it over and over again.

- Ask them what increases when something is practiced.

PROCESSING: This handout provides a great way to understand the flow of information at the neuronal level of the brain. Discuss the fact that the flow gets faster and more efficient the more it happens—as they probably noticed when they did the exercise—with practice.

The HAND/ARM model of a NEURON

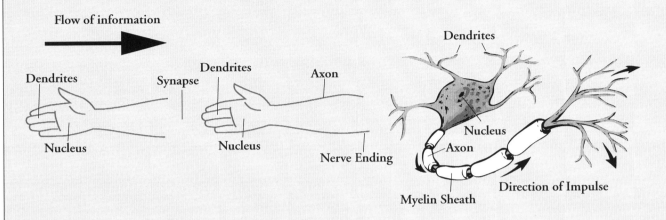

- Nerve cells, or **neurons**, carry messages through electrochemical impulses or signals. As neurons fire, the number and size of dendrites increase.
- **Dendrites** are branched projections of a neuron that conduct electrochemical information received from other neural cells to the cell body from which the dendrites project.
- **Axons** are long projections from a neuron that conduct electrical impulses away from the cell body to the nerve endings.
- **Nerve endings** transmit information to other neurons across the synapse.
- The **synapse** permits a neuron to pass an electrical or chemical signal to another cell.

EXERCISE
- Pretend your left hand has dendrites, which receive messages.
- Your torso is the cell body.
- Your right arm is the axon.
- Your right hand represents nerve endings.
- Pretend a coin (rock, pencil, eraser) is the message.
- Place the coin in your left hand, and then pass it to your right hand.
- Pass the "message" from person to person across the gap between your hands (the synapse) in this way.
- Does this get easier and faster with practice?
- How is that like the brain?

Tool 2-19: Draw a Picture of Your Brain in Your Journal

THEORY: Drawing a picture of basic brain structures can reinforce the understanding of how mindfulness practice improves the structure and function of the brain. This tool helps clients apply what they have learned about this by drawing a picture of the brain.

IMPLEMENTATION: Ask clients to draw a basic picture of their brain in their journal. Use Handout 2-19 to help them. Ask them to list what the different brain structures do. Encourage them to reference the previous handouts on brain structure as needed.

PROCESSING: Review the functions of the brain structures relevant to mindfulness. Review the client's picture. Answer their questions and clarify the location and function of the brain structures.

HANDOUT 2-19
DRAW A PICTURE OF YOUR BRAIN

Draw a picture of your brain in your journal. Include the following structures. Make a note about what function each structure is responsible for.

STRUCTURES

- Prefrontal Cortex
- Amygdala
- Insula
- Parietal Lobes
- Occipital Lobes
- Temporal Lobes

FUNCTIONS

- Security Guard
- Conductor
- Interoception
- Sensory Integration
- Visual Processing
- Auditory Processing and Emotional Regulation

TOOLS FOR EXPLAINING THE RESEARCH

Tool 2-20: Explain Mindfulness Research

THEORY: Many clients become more invested in mindfulness practice when they discover that there is a significant body of research that shows the benefits of mindfulness. This tool provides a quick summary of the research, which gives mindfulness more credibility and helps clients understand why they should incorporate it into their lives

IMPLEMENTATION: Review research Handout 2-20. Ask the client to make a list of the benefits that mindfulness research proves might help them.

PROCESSING: At this point some clients may still be struggling to understand the benefits of mindfulness and "what's in it for me?" This tool shows them the broad range of benefits of mindfulness. Help clients begin to relate how benefits gained from mindfulness practice apply to their own life and the issues they are dealing with.

HANDOUT 2-20
SUMMARY OF MINDFULNESS RESEARCH

Research on mindful meditation's effect on the MIND:

- Meditation practice is associated with **lower levels of psychological distress, including less anxiety, depression, anger, and worry** (cf. Baer, 2003; Brown, Ryan, & Creswell, 2007; Greeson & Brantley, in press; Grossman et al., 2004).

- Formal meditation practices (body scan, yoga, sitting meditation) at home during an 8-week intervention led to increased mindfulness, which, in turn, explained **decreased psychological distress and increased psychological well-being** (Carmody & Baer, 2008).

- Four weeks of mindfulness meditation training reduced distress by **decreasing rumination**, a cognitive process associated with depression and other mood disorders (Jain et al., 2007). Another clinical study found that 8 weeks of mindfulness meditation training significantly **reduced ruminative thinking** in persons with a history of depression (Ramel et al., 2004).

- Simply being in a mindful state momentarily is associated with a **greater sense of well-being** (Lau et al., 2006).

- Research has found that people with higher natural levels of mindfulness—irrespective of formal meditation training—report **feeling less stressed, anxious and depressed, and more joyful, inspired, grateful, hopeful, content, vital, and satisfied with life** (Baer et al., 2006; Brown & Ryan, 2003; Cardaciotto et al., 2008; Feldman et al., 2007; Walach et al., 2006).

- Research suggests that people with higher levels of mindfulness are better able to regulate their sense of well-being by virtue of **greater emotional awareness, understanding, acceptance, and the ability to correct or repair unpleasant mood states** (Baer et al., 2008; cf. Brown, Ryan, & Creswell, 2007; Feldman et al., 2007). The ability to skillfully regulate one's internal emotional experience in the present moment may **translate into good mental health long-term.**

- Mindfulness-based training programs—including Mindfulness-Based Stress Reduction (MBSR), Mindfulness-Based Cognitive Therapy (MBCT), Acceptance and Commitment Therapy (ACT), Dialectical Behavior Therapy (DBT), and Mindfulness-Based Eating Awareness Training (MB-EAT)—can effectively treat more **serious mental health conditions, including anxiety disorders** (MBSR; ACT), **recurrent major depression** (MBCT), **chronic pain** (MBSR; ACT**), borderline personality disorder** (DBT), and **binge eating disorder** (MB-EAT) (Baer, 2006).

Research on mindful meditation's effect on the BRAIN:

- A number of studies have demonstrated that systematic mindfulness training, as well as brief meditation practices in novices, can influence areas of the brain involved in **regulating attention, awareness, and emotion** (cf. Cahn & Policy, 2006; Lutz et al., 2008a).

- A clinical study found that 8 weeks of mindfulness meditation training (MBSR) led to an **increased ability to orient one's attention to the present moment, as measured by a laboratory attention test** (Jha, Krompinger, & Baime, 2007).

- One study found that compared to a relaxation training control group, 5 days of integrative meditation training—including mindfulness—**significantly improved the efficiency of executive attention during a computerized attention test** (Tang et al., 2007). **Good news for ADHD!**

- Another study found that employees in a corporate setting **showed changes in front brain electrical activity (EEG)** following 8 weeks of MBSR that were **consistent with the experience of positive emotions like joy and content** (Davidson et al., 2003).

- One functional magnetic resonance imaging (MRI) study found that 8 weeks of MBSR was **associated with greater neural activity in two brain regions believed to partially subserve self-awareness—the dorsolateral PFC and the medial PFC**—during experiential and narrative self-focus tasks, respectively (Farb et al., 2007).

- A structural MRI study reported that experienced mindfulness meditators, relative to demographically matched controls, had **increased grey matter in brain regions that are typically activated during meditation, such as the right anterior insula, which subserves interoceptive awareness** (Hölzel et al., 2007a).

- In adept meditators versus non-meditators, mindful breathing practice (contrasted to mental arithmetic) was associated with **increased rostral ACC and dorsomedial PFC activation, which may reflect stronger processing of distracting events and emotions**, respectively (Hölzel et al., 2007b).

- A 2011 study led by Massachusetts General Hospital researchers published in *Psychiatry Research: Neuroimaging* (January 30, 2011)
  - **Increased grey-matter density in the hippocampus**, known to be **important for learning and memory**, and in structures associated with **self-awareness, compassion, and introspection**.
  - Participant-reported reductions in stress also were correlated with **decreased grey-matter density in the amygdala**, which is known to play an **important role in anxiety and stress**.

- Richard Davidson et al. (2003) carried out by J. Kabat-Zinn
  - Consisted of weekly meetings of approximately 3 hours to practice meditation, a silent retreat during the sixth week, and homework including the practice of meditation for 1 hour every day, 6 days a week.
  - EEG was recorded: before treatment, immediately after the treatment, and 4 months after that.
  - The EEG data were used to obtain a measurement of the cerebral activation of each hemisphere, right and left, which in its turn was used to calculate the degree of asymmetry existing between the two sides.
  - The activation of the zone under study is inversely related to the power of the alpha band (8-13 Hz). In other words the lower the power of the alpha band, the greater the cerebral activation, and vice-versa.
  - Davidson et al. found that the meditators, in comparison to the non-meditators, experienced a **greater increase in left cerebral activation** in the anterior and median zones, a pattern associated with the presence of a positive affective disposition.

- SPECT (Single Photon Emission Computed Tomography) scan—**study found cerebral blood flow differences between long-term meditators and non-meditators** (Newberg et al., 2010).
  - The CBF (cerebral blood flow) of long-term meditators was significantly higher compared to non-meditators in the prefrontalcortex, parietal cortex, thalamus, putamen, caudate, and midbrain. There was also a significant difference in the thalamic laterality, with long-term meditators having greater asymmetry. The observed changes associated with long-term meditation appear in structures that underlie the attention network and also those that relate to emotion and autonomic functions.

- A functional brain imaging study found that practicing a brief loving kindness meditation **activated regions of the brain associated with positive feelings toward others** (Hutcherson, Seppala, & Gross, 2008).

- Loving kindness meditation—traditionally included as part of mindfulness training—is a contemplative practice designed to **foster acceptance and compassion for oneself and others** (Kabat-Zinn, 1990; The Dalai Lama, 2001).

- A feasibility study titled "Mindfulness Meditation Training in Adults and Adolescents With ADHD" published in the *Journal of Attention Disorders* found that **meditation led to improvements in self-reported ADHD symptoms and test performance on tasks measuring attention and cognitive inhibition. Improvements in anxiety and depressive symptoms** so common in people with ADHD were also observed (Zylowska, L., et al, 2008).

- Overall, it appears that **focused, concentrative meditation practices can increase one's ability to maintain steady attention on a chosen object**, like the breath or another person, whereas **open awareness meditation practices can increase one's ability to flexibly monitor and redirect attention when it becomes distracted** (Lutz et al., 2008a).

Research on mindful meditation's effect on the BODY:

- Scientific evidence to support the therapeutic effect of mindfulness meditation training on stress-related medical conditions, including **psoriasis** (Kabat-Zinn et al., 1998), **type 2 diabetes** (Rosenzweig et al., 2007), **fibromyalgia** (Grossman et al., 2007), **rheumatoid arthritis** (Pradhan et al., 2007; Zautra et al., 2008**), chronic low back pain** (Morone, Greco & Weiner, 2008), and **attention-deficit hyperactivity disorder** (Zylowska et al., 2008).

- Research has consistently shown that mindfulness training **reduces symptoms of stress and negative mood states and increases emotional well-being and quality of life, among persons with chronic illness** (cf. Brown, Ryan, & Creswell, 2007; Grossman et al., 2004; Ludwig & Kabat-Zinn, 2008; Shigaki, Glass, & Schopp, 2006).

- Eight-week MBSR study by Davidson and colleagues (2003) showed that **individuals who had the largest shifts in frontal brain activity also had the strongest antibody responses to a flu vaccine**. That study was the first to show that mindfulness training can change the brain and the immune system in a way that might bolster resistance to disease.

Research on mindfulness effect on BEHAVIOR:

- Some of the studies to date have found that people trained in mindfulness show a **better ability to quit smoking** (Davis et al., 2007), **decrease binge eating** (Kristeller, Baer, & Quillian-Wolever, 2006), and **reduce alcohol and illicit substance use** (Bowen et al., 2006).

- Mindfulness may also promote better health, in part, by **improving sleep quality**, which can be disrupted by stress, anxiety, and difficulty turning off the mind (Winbush Kreitzer, 2007).

Tool 2-21: Connect Mindfulness Research with Benefits for Client's Condition

THEORY: Despite the fact that mindfulness can effectively improve many different conditions, some clients are very skeptical about it. Use this tool to help them understand how the scientific research suggests that practicing mindfulness might help their specific condition. This tool helps the client to "buy in" to using mindfulness and opens their receptivity to trying it.

IMPLEMENTATION: With the client look through the Summary of Mindfulness Research in Handout 2-20 and find some that pertain to the condition(s) the client is dealing with. Help them understand how mindfulness practice might be beneficial for them. Ask them if they would be willing to learn some mindfulness exercises like those done in the studies if it would decrease their symptoms. This helps them make a commitment to giving this a try.

PROCESSING: Explore client understanding of how mindfulness may be helpful to them. Answer questions. Give examples from research and from your practice. This is a good time to write treatment goals with the client. List the specific symptoms they want to improve that mindfulness might positively impact. See Tools 22-1 and 22-2 for guidance on defining treatment goals and tracking progress. This sets up the process for monitoring progress and helps ensure accountability during the therapeutic process.

Tool 2-22: Journal About Why Mindfulness Helps People with Your Condition

THEORY: Starting a new skill such as mindfulness is a change process for most clients. Writing about how mindfulness works, how it changes the brain, and how this helps specific conditions the client is dealing with will assist the client in understanding the benefits they might experience from mindfulness.

IMPLEMENTATION:

Journal Prompts:

- List the conditions you need help with, such as depression, anxiety, well-being, concentration, sleep, specific medical condition, stress management, etc.
- List the parts of the brain that mindfulness affects that may help with your condition.
- Do you know anyone who has incorporated mindfulness into their life and if yes, what benefits have they experienced?
- What would keep your from using mindfulness?
- Do you believe mindfulness can help you?
- How would you feel if mindfulness improved the symptoms of your condition?

PROCESSING: Review the client's journal entries with them. Help them connect their condition with the mindfulness research and neurobiology that pertains to their condition. Give them some examples from your practice or your reading about others who have the same condition and who have been helped with mindfulness. Address any resistance or obstacles that they present. Use the tools in Chapter 4 under "How to Identify and Overcome Obstacles and Resistance."

Chapter 3: Tools to Increase Client Use of Mindfulness at Home

Tool 3-1: How to Find a Comfortable Position

THEORY: When practicing a sitting mindfulness meditation, the client will be maintaining their physical position for anywhere from a few minutes to 20 minutes. Therefore it is important to help them find a position they can comfortably maintain for the duration of their practice. Discomfort will distract them from their meditation. Positions range from a basic sitting position in a chair to the Full Lotus position. Some clients may find it impossible to sit for any length of time and in this case a walking meditation may be most suitable.

This tool introduces the client to several possible positions and helps them select the one(s) that work best for them. The position of the hands is also included in this tool.

IMPLEMENTATION: Review Handouts 3-1A and 3-1B with the client, show them how to do each position, watch them do it, and make suggestions to help them get comfortable. Suggest they sit on a cushion or meditation stool when sitting cross legged. Then ask them to try each position while practicing various mindfulness skills. Help them select the position that works best for them.

PROCESSING: Assist the client in finding the position(s) that works best for them. After they try each position, ask them what they noticed about their body. Was it comfortable? Were they able to relax? Was it hard to stay in that position? Did they have trouble staying still? Did they have the urge to change positions?

Also ask them what they noticed about their mindfulness in each position. Were they distracted by body sensations? Were they able to stay focused on their intended mindfulness target such as breath? Did their hand position change anything about their practice? How did the walking meditation impact their mindfulness?

SITTING IN A CHAIR

Sit in a chair with feet flat on the floor, back straight, and palms turned upward resting lightly on your lap. You may lean back against the back of the chair for support as long as you keep your back straight.

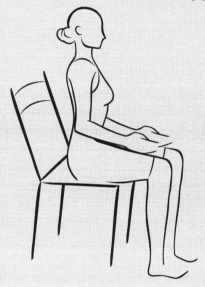

LYING DOWN

Lie flat on your back with arms and legs uncrossed, arms lying by your side with palms up. You may place a pillow under your head and perhaps under your knees for comfort.

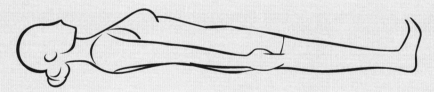

SITTING WITH CROSSED LEGS

Sit with legs crossed, palms face up on your knees. You may sit on a small pillow or meditation stool for comfort.

FULL LOTUS POSITION

The Lotus Position is the ultimate meditation pose. It requires flexibility in the knees and can take years of practice to attain. Sit with both knees folded with each foot placed up on the thighs and palms placed upward on the thighs. Do not worry if you cannot do this. Just use the cross-legged position instead. But if you can, go for it.

WALKING

Walk with arms swinging freely at your sides, body upright, eyes looking ahead, hands unclenched, and shoulders relaxed.

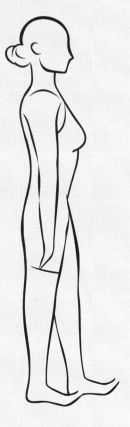

TOUCH THUMB AND FOREFINGER IN A CIRCLE.

Chin or Pran Mudrā: Join the thumb and forefinger on each of both hands as a zero. Extend the rest of the fingers, with the middle finger touching the non-folded part of the forefinger. Place the hands palms-up on the thighs while sitting.

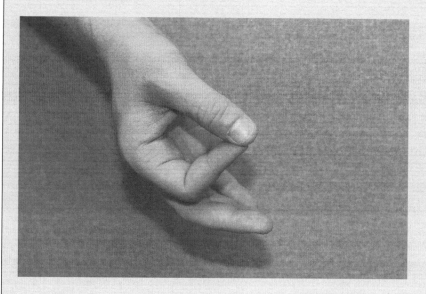

TOUCH THUMB AND MIDDLE FINGER TOGETHER IN A CIRCLE.

Healing Mudra: Join thumb and middle finger to form a circle. Extend the rest of the fingers. Place the hands palms-up on the thighs while sitting.

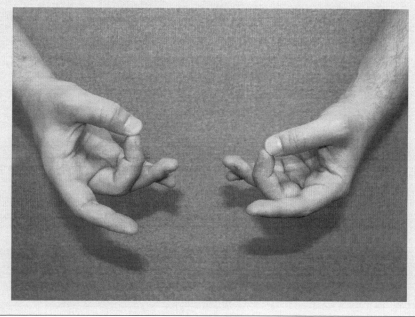

Tool 3-2: How to Find a Time That Works and Schedule It

THEORY: Most people find that the best way to ensure they incorporate mindfulness into their daily life is to set aside a specific time each day to practice. "Fitting it in" rarely works for most people. This applies to formal sitting mindfulness meditation as well as mindfulness practices that can be integrated into daily activities. There is no one best time to meditate. Some people prefer first thing in the morning before the daily demands start as a way to set up for a great day. Others prefer the end of the day as a way to "unwind" before sleep. The goal of this tool is to help clients deliberately choose a time and commit to making it work for them.

IMPLEMENTATION:

Formal Sitting Mindfulness Meditations

Ask your client to think about their current daily schedule. You might need to suggest they use a planner and schedule time for themselves. Help them find a time that they could set aside 10 to 15 minutes at the same time every day. For some people this might be first thing in the morning before they start their morning routine. For others this might be after the kids are on the bus and before they leave for work. Still others may find that closing the door to their office for 15 minutes as soon as they arrive at work is the best time. Some people find that taking a break for themselves during their lunchtime works well. Another favorite time is at night just before going to bed when the household is settled in for the night. Ask them to choose a time and fill it in on Handout 3-2.

Mindfulness Practice During Daily Activities

Explain to your client that many of the mindfulness tools in this workbook are designed to be incorporated while doing the activities of the day. For example, the Awareness of Surroundings (Tool 6-1) can be used at any time but is particularly helpful upon arrival in a new environment. You will be teaching this skill to your client later on. But for now tell them to stop, breathe, and notice their surroundings periodically throughout their day. Use Handout 3-2 to help them choose when they will practice this tool.

The Mindfulness of Tasks Tool 11-2 is specifically designed to be practiced while doing a task. This task might be driving, eating, doing the dishes, taking a shower, using the restroom, doing a work project, or any commonly performed task. Help your client use the handout to pick two tasks during which they will intend to be mindful using the Mindfulness of Tasks tool. These can be scheduled throughout their day.

PROCESSING: Help your client deliberately think about when they will incorporate mindfulness into their day and commit to doing it then. This will greatly increase the chances that they will actually practice it. At each session, ask them when they practiced and help them fine-tune the best time for them. Many clients will raise objections, stating that they simply don't have time. Use Tool 4-7a to help them overcome this objection.

HANDOUT 3-2
SCHEDULING TIME TO PRACTICE MINDFULNESS

FORMAL SITTING MINDFULNESS MEDITATIONS

- Think about your current daily schedule.

- Find a time to set aside 10 to 15 minutes at the same time every day.
    - first thing in the morning before you start your morning routine
    - after the kids are on the bus and before you leave for work
    - for 15 minutes as soon as you arrive at work
    - during lunchtime
    - during a break at work
    - at night just before going to bed when the household is settled in for the night
    - I intend to practice my formal sitting mindfulness at:
      _____ o'clock each day.

MINDFULNESS PRACTICE DURING DAILY ACTIVITIES

- Many of the mindfulness tools are designed to be incorporated as you go through the activities of your day. For example, Awareness of Surroundings (Tool 6-1) can be used at any time but is particularly helpful when you:
    - arrive in a new environment
    - get to work
    - go into a store
    - climb in the car
    - walk into the house
    - go anyplace else during the day
    - I intend to be mindful of my surroundings in these two places:
      1.) _____   2.) _____

- The Awareness of Tasks Mindfulness (Tool 11-2) is specifically designed to be practiced while you are doing a task. This task might be
    - driving
    - eating
    - doing the dishes
    - taking a shower or using the restroom
    - doing a work project or homework
    - any task you commonly perform
    - I intend to be mindful while doing these two tasks every day:
      1.) _____   2.) _____

Tool 3-3: How to Find a Place for Core Practice

THEORY: Setting aside a specific location for regularly scheduled core sitting meditation practice helps the client associate that place with mindfulness, which helps them relax into the meditation more quickly. Carefully choosing a place can ensure both comfort and fewer distractions. Generally, this will make it easier to practice. It is certainly acceptable to practice anywhere and for some clients this works great. But setting up a suitable space is very important for most clients.

IMPLEMENTATION: Use Handout 3-3 to help your client make a list of potential practice locations. Help them identify and eliminate potential sources of distraction such as phones, TVs, street noise, family demands, and temperature. Assist them in setting up a space that is calming, soothing, and pleasing to them.

PROCESSING: Now that your client has gone through the process of choosing and setting up a space, ask them how it is working out for them. Help them fine-tune it, if necessary. If they have resisted doing this step and are not having success with their practice, encourage them to complete this step to see for themselves how it changes their practice.

FIND A PLACE FOR CORE MINDFULNESS PRACTICE

- List the elements of a suitable place. This might include:
    - quiet
    - comfortable temperature
    - soothing lighting
    - calming décor
    - pictures that are soothing
    - candles or incense (avoid if allergic)
    - free of distractions such as phones, TV, family demands, noise
    - easily accessible
    - convenient
    - inside
    - outside in a natural setting
- Make a list of possible locations for your practice.

Location	Pros	Cons

- List the pros and cons of each place (above).
- List what you might do to make the space more appealing.

- Choose and try out your top two locations.
    - 1.) _____   2.) _____

Tool 3-4: How to Incorporate Mindfulness into Daily Activities

THEORY: Mindfulness practice will never be effective if clients don't actually do it. This workbook provides many mindfulness tools that can be incorporated directly into daily life. Some are considered formal sitting meditations. Others are mindfulness tools that the client can use as they do tasks throughout the day. One significant goal of mindfulness is to increase "awareness of awareness" on a moment-to-moment basis throughout the day. The more formal sitting mindfulness meditation skills train this "awareness of awareness" skill. Then, this skill can be applied actively throughout the day using tools such as Mindfulness of Breath (Tool 5-5), Mindfulness of Surroundings (Tools 6-1 and 6-2), Mindfulness of Tasks (Tools 11-1 and 11-2), and Mindfulness of Intention (Tools 13-1, 13-2, and 13-3).

IMPLEMENTATION:

Help the client incorporate mindfulness practice into their daily life.

- Help them establish a **time and place** for regular sitting practice.
- As you teach your client the specific mindfulness tools, help them **choose styles** that work best for them.
- Show them how to **practice mindfulness outside of sitting meditations**.
  - Mindfulness of Breath (Chapter 5)
  - Present Moment Awareness (Chapter 6)
  - Mindfulness of Tasks (Chapter 11)
  - Mindfulness of Intention (Chapter 13)
  - Mindfulness of Motion (Chapter 15)
- **Start small** and gradually increase little by little.
- Help them **commit** to the practice.
- Explain how and why to give practice **priority**.
- Teach them how to **monitor progress** (Chapter 22).

PROCESSING: Discuss the importance of incorporating mindfulness into everyday life. Ask the client when they used both sitting and active mindfulness. Ask them when they might have used it but didn't. Explore their commitment to using mindfulness. Discuss what they expect to get out of it. Explore the importance of giving it priority.

Tool 3-5: Journaling About Your Plans to Use Mindfulness

THEORY: As with any new practice it is important to clarify and understand personal expectations and commitment. This journaling tool will help the client explore their personal motivation and commitment to this work.

IMPLEMENTATION: Ask your client to review the journal prompts in Handout 3-5 and to respond to as many as they can. Explain that starting any new practice requires commitment, time, and energy and that these journal prompts will help them clarify their commitment and intention.

PROCESSING: Explore what came up for the client when they answered these prompts. Encourage them to make a clear commitment. If they are hesitant, explore their concerns and address objections using Tools 4-7 through 4-8. Ask them to start small with one basic mindfulness tool such as Belly Breathing (Tool 5-2), Awareness of Breath (Tool 5-5), or Present Moment Awareness (Tools in Chapter 6). Keep it simple and make it easy.

HANDOUT 3-5
JOURNALING ABOUT YOUR PLANS TO USE MINDFULNESS

Journal Prompts:

- Why do you want to learn and use mindfulness skills?
- When have you been mindful this week?
- Where and when will you practice sitting mindfulness meditation?
- What benefits do you hope to gain from mindfulness practice?
- What hesitations do you feel about doing this practice?
- What physical positions work best for you?
- How much time are you willing to commit to mindfulness practice?
- How important is this practice to you?
- What would you be willing to give up doing in order to make time to practice?
- What would you rather be doing?
- Are you surprised that there is more to mindfulness than sitting meditations?
- What are you most looking forward to about this practice?

Chapter 4: Tools for Teaching Mindfulness Basics

EXPLAIN THE BASIC PROCESS OF MINDFULNESS

Tool 4-1: Notice, Accept, Dismiss, Return

THEORY: The basis of mindfulness is to focus on something in particular, the chosen target of attention, and to return attention to that target whenever attention wanders. This tool provides two simple ways to explain the process to your client.

IMPLEMENTATION: Explain to your client that the goal of mindfulness is not to have a mind that is totally empty of thoughts. With 60,000 thoughts a day, it is perfectly normal to have some thoughts while practicing mindfulness. Instead, the goal is to first choose something to focus attention on and then to notice distracted thoughts and emotions as they arise, to accept them, to let them go, and then to return attention to the chosen target of attention. Over and over again. Give your client a copy of Handout 4-1 to remind them of this process. Encourage them to practice. Explain that this is the basis of all mindfulness skills. Make sure they understand that they can apply this process to thoughts, emotions, physical sensations, and distractions in the environment that arise during mindfulness practice.

PROCESSING: Explore with your client how they are doing with this process. How does it feel to know that being mindful does not mean they have an empty mind? Are they able to notice thoughts as they arise? What emotions or physical sensations have they noticed during practice? How are they returning their attention to their target of attention? Is it getting easier with practice?

HANDOUT 4-1
NOTICE, ACCEPT, DISMISS, RETURN

Use the following to remind you of the basic process of mindfulness.

Choose something to focus on. This might be your breath, your surroundings, a mantra, a sound, a physical sensation, a concept, or a task. This will be your "target of attention."

Focus your attention on your target. Every time you notice that your mind has wandered, use the following process to **Notice** the thought, **Accept** it without judgment, **Dismiss** the thought without engaging in it, and **Return** your attention back to your chosen target of attention. Notice, accept, dismiss, return, and repeat. Repeat this process throughout your mindfulness practice.

NOTICE
ACCEPT
DISMISS
RETURN
REPEAT

Another easy way to remember this process is with the acronym **SOLAR**: **S**top. **O**bserve the thought without judgment. **L**et the thought go without engaging in it. **A**nd **R**eturn your attention to your chosen target.

Stop
Observe
Let It Go
And
Return

DOING THE EXERCISES WITH YOUR CLIENT

Tool 4-2: Find an Opening to Introduce Concept in Session

THEORY: Mindfulness practice may be quite new to most clients. Knowing when and how to introduce mindfulness skills to the client in session so that they embrace them can be tricky. This tool provides guidance on how to comfortably and appropriately introduce mindfulness concepts.

IMPLEMENTATION: First and foremost you need to practice mindfulness yourself before teaching it to your clients. Your own practice will ensure that you recognize when issues that could benefit from mindfulness practice present themselves in session. Let clients know how mindfulness practice has helped you or other clients with issues like theirs. See Tools 4-9 through 4-14 for information on how to get the client to "buy into" using mindfulness.

With individual clients, simply integrate mindfulness skills into your work with them. Look for an opening to present itself during a session where you can suggest that mindfulness skills might help the client with a particular condition. For example, if a client is experiencing anxiety, tell them you would like to show them a way to help them lower and gain control over their anxiety and then teach them to belly breathe (Tool 5-2). Or lead them in a progressive relaxation meditation or recommend they listen to a meditation CD. If they have trouble concentrating, teach them the SOLAR concept to train themselves to stay on task (Tool 4-1). Mindfulness skills will help clients with most issues so you will find plenty of opportunities to introduce it. Review Section IV for ideas on how to use mindfulness to treat specific disorders.

Depending on the client, you may tell them you think they could benefit from learning mindfulness skills, or you might just teach them individual skills without necessarily calling it mindfulness or meditation. The word "meditation" often puts people off as they picture sitting still for long periods and feel they could never do that. They may not realize that they can incorporate mindfulness right into their day as they walk, work, or do their chores.

Obviously it's easier to introduce mindfulness if you are facilitating a "mindfulness or meditation" group as the clients already know the focus of the group. Other types of groups also benefit from mindfulness. Talk to the group participants about incorporating mindfulness skills into the group sessions.

PROCESSING: How did your client react when you introduced mindfulness? Did they object? If so, review the section on how to overcome obstacles and resistance (Tools 4-6 through 4-8). What did they like about it? How was it helpful? Are they willing to learn more skills? Will they agree to practice at home or only in the session? Were you able to explain the benefits?

Tool 4-3: Assign Mindfulness Skill Practice

THEORY: In order to achieve the benefits of mindfulness, the skills must be practiced and incorporated into daily life. This tool reviews the process for encouraging clients to practice them at home.

IMPLEMENTATION: Explain that mindfulness skills need to be practiced and incorporated into the client's daily routine in order to work. After teaching any specific skill in session, encourage the client to practice it at home, work, or at school. Ask them when they think they might do it and help them find time if they don't know. Discuss what might get in the way and options for overcoming obstacles. Help them brainstorm about when and where they can practice the skill. For example, if you are teaching Mindfulness of Surroundings (Tools 6-1 and 6-2), suggest they might stop, breathe, and notice their surroundings every day when they first arrive at work. Or if you are teaching Mindfulness of Tasks (Tools 11-1 and 11-2), pick a specific task during which they will practice mindfulness. This might be as simple as while brushing their teeth or loading the dishwasher. Choose something they do every day.

PROCESSING: Did the client understand how to do the skill? Were they willing to practice at home? Were you able to help them find a time and place for practice? How did you feel assigning them "homework." Think about how you will feel if they don't follow through. How might they feel if they don't practice?

PROCESS WHAT HAPPENS WITH YOUR CLIENT

Tool 4-4: What Happened During and After Practice?

THEORY: After assigning a specific skill for home practice, it is important to explore what happened when the client tried it. This helps them overcome obstacles and ensures they will find skills that work best for them. It will help their practice become more effective as you help them fine-tune it. It also provides opportunities for helping them explore their feelings and for helping them therapeutically. This tool provides guidance on how to help the client process their experience.

IMPLEMENTATION: Ask the client, "So, were you able to practice the skill?" If they were, then ask them: When did you do it? What happened when you did it? How did it go? Did you feel like you were able to do it like we discussed or did you do it differently? How did you feel? Were you comfortable doing it? Did anything negative happen? What got in your way? How did it help? Do you have any questions about it? How can you adjust it to work better?

Sadly, many clients will say, "No, I forgot to do it," or "I didn't have time," or any number of other excuses. That's okay. Use the next tool, Tool 4-5, to handle this situation.

PROCESSING: Help your client examine their overall experience doing the practice. Answer questions. Help them fine-tune their practice depending on how it went. Suggest other skills that might work better for them.

Tool 4-5: What to Do if a Client Didn't Practice?

THEORY: Sadly, many clients will not follow through on their practice. They will say, "I forgot to do it," or "I didn't have time," or any number of other excuses. That's okay. This tool helps you handle the situation when the client didn't practice.

IMPLEMENTATION: If the client did not practice the assigned skill, say, "That's okay. When might you have practiced the skill?" Then help them identify a time they might have done it. Explore why they didn't practice and what got in their way. If they forgot, ask them what they could do this week to remember. If they raised other objections, see Tools 4-7 and 4-8 for how to handle common objections. Be sure to do it with them in session.

PROCESSING: Ask your client what prevented them from practicing. Explore how they are feeling about trying this skill. Explore their objections. Address their fears or concerns. Remind them of the benefits. Help them identify when they might have practiced and also when they were being mindful without realizing it.

HOW TO IDENTIFY AND OVERCOME OBSTACLES AND RESISTANCE

Tool 4-6: How to Recognize Common Obstacles

THEORY: As with learning any new skill, clients may experience resistance and discover obstacles that prevent them from practicing. That's okay. This tool helps you be prepared for this to happen and helps you recognize it when it does.

IMPLEMENTATION: Some of the common obstacles include:

- I didn't have time.
- I can't stay focused, so why bother?
- I don't know how to do it right.
- This doesn't work for me.
- I fell asleep.
- Mindfulness is too religious for me.
- I feel silly doing this.
- It's boring.
- I don't see how this could possibly help me.

PROCESSING: Be prepared to hear about many obstacles that get in the way of the client's being able to practice. The next step is to process these excuses with the client to help them resolve them. See Tool 4-7 for ideas on how to address each of these.

Tool 4-7: Address Objections with Client

THEORY: Many people will have trouble following through with mindfulness practice. This tool provides guidance on how to handle some common objections.

IMPLEMENTATION:

a. I didn't have time.   People are busy these days. And, at first, many clients feel that mindfulness is a waste of time and they should use the time to get stuff done.

Remind them that it doesn't take any time at all to practice being mindful while brushing teeth or taking a shower or driving. It just takes a small commitment to doing it and something to remind them to do it.

Yes, the sitting meditations do take time, anywhere from a few minutes to 15 or 20 minutes. In order for the client to be willing to set aside the time, help them really understand what the likely benefits will be.

b. I forgot.   It is not unusual to forget to practice mindfulness as the busyness of life takes over. Review the benefits of mindfulness and help the client make a commitment to practicing. Help them find a way to remind themselves to be mindful. Perhaps they can put a sticky note on the bathroom mirror, or on the steering wheel. Help them set aside time on a regular basis and put it in their electronic planner with an alarm to remind them.

c. I can't stay focused, so why bother?   Explain that it is perfectly normal for thoughts to wander. The goal is to notice those thoughts, dismiss them, and bring attention back to the mindfulness practice. Over and over again. It gets easier with practice but even skilled mindfulness practitioners must still do this.

d. I don't know how to do it right, so it won't help. Discuss how they are doing it and why they don't think it is right. Explain that there is no one "right" way to practice mindfulness. Help them find the ways that work best for them and that they feel confident doing.

e. This doesn't work for me. Clients often say, "I've tried this before and it doesn't work for me." This is the opening for you to ask them what they have tried before and what happened when they did it. There are so many different ways to practice mindfulness it is highly unlikely that there aren't some that work for each client. The only mindfulness technique many clients have heard of is formal sitting meditation. They may have attempted to sit still for 20 minutes without thinking about anything and found this intolerable. That's okay. Explain about the other options and find some that suit the client. Start small and work up.

f. I fell asleep. Many clients report that they fall asleep when they meditate. Many are exhausted, sleep-deprived, and running on empty, so it's no surprise that if they sit quietly for a few minutes and start to relax, they fall asleep. There are several ways to approach this. First, address why they are so tired and help them find ways to reduce their fatigue. This might include everything from helping them improve their sleep hygiene to encouraging them to take a nap. The second way to approach this is to tell them that it's okay to sleep; that if they are that tired, then sleep is probably what they need most. For some, this takes the pressure off and, as they address their sleep deficit, they gradually become more able to stay awake. The third approach is to help them make a commitment to staying awake while they meditate. Help them make this a priority. Perhaps they could do a walking meditation instead of a sitting meditation so they don't fall asleep. Maybe they could choose a position that doesn't support sleeping such as kneeling or sitting on a chair with no back. Perhaps they can choose a time to meditate when they are not so tired.

g. It's too religious for me. It's true that mindfulness meditation has its roots in Eastern traditions and Buddhism. But Jon Kabat-Zinn brought the skills and practice of mindfulness into the mainstream over 20 years ago. The mindfulness skills taught here are not based in religion and are practiced by those of any or no faith. They can be used in a religious context, but the approach we use for clients is non-secular.

h. I feel silly doing this. Many people feel silly sitting, closing their eyes, and doing the mindfulness practice. Explore what feels silly about it and options for making them feel more comfortable. One option is to do it with them in session. Another is to help them find a private place to practice so they avoid embarrassment or judgment.

i. It's boring. Many clients report that they feel bored when they first try to meditate. That's okay. Explore options for making their practice less boring. This might include trying a different mindfulness skill or finding an interesting focus for their attention. It may also include helping them tolerate the boredom by shortening the time to a tolerable length and gradually increasing it as their tolerance improves. Moving or walking meditations tend to be more tolerable for clients with ADHD or for those who feel bored or anxious just sitting still.

j. I don't see how this could possibly help me. Review the benefits proven by the research that apply to this client. Explain how mindfulness works and how it helps their condition. Ask them to trust the process and give it a try before rejecting it out of hand. If they cannot do so, this may not yet be the time to incorporate mindfulness into their life. Everyone is on their own journey. As helpers we can only give people options. It is up to them to decide what they will do.

PROCESSING: Explore the objections raised by your client to help them overcome them. Discuss options for making a commitment to practice. When assigning a new skill, explore how they will overcome their objections and practice the skill this time.

Tool 4-8: Journal About Your Objections and How to Overcome Them

THEORY: Journaling about their experiences with learning new mindfulness skills will help clients address their objections and raise their awareness about the process (which in itself is a mindfulness exercise). This tool provides prompts that guide clients through this self-awareness process.

IMPLEMENTATION: Give Handout 4-8 to clients and ask them to write or verbally answer the prompts.

PROCESSING: Review the answers with clients. What did they learn about themselves through answering the prompts? What objections do they still have? How are they overcoming these objections?

HANDOUT 4-8
JOURNAL ABOUT YOUR OBJECTIONS AND HOW TO OVERCOME THEM

Journal Prompts:

- What objections do (or did) you have about doing this mindfulness practice?
- Are these objections connected to anything else such as ADHD, anxiety, depression, trauma, or previous experience with practice?
- What are you doing to handle and overcome your objections?
- Do you feel you can overcome them?
- Can you practice mindfulness despite your objections?
- Are there any objections that are "show stoppers" that will prevent you from practicing mindfulness?
- Have you noticed these objections in other areas of your life?
- List three benefits you expect from mindfulness practice.

TOOLS FOR GETTING CLIENTS TO BUY INTO USING MINDFULNESS

Tool 4-9: What Do They Know About It?

THEORY: When introducing mindfulness to any client, it is important to understand what they already know about it. This process helps you know where to start to teach mindfulness skills to this client. This tool describes the process as well as pitfalls to be aware of.

IMPLEMENTATION: When introducing mindfulness to clients, first ask them if they know what mindfulness is. Ask them if they have practiced mindfulness before and if so exactly what they did. Explore how what they did before compares with the mindfulness skills you want to teach them. Be wary when they tell you they've done it before and it doesn't work for them or that they already know all about it. Go deeper to explore exactly what they did and why it did or didn't work for them. This will help you discover how what they've tried may differ from what you are teaching. It will also give you more information about what might work best for this particular client, what their objections may be, and where to begin.

One young boy told me he knew how to breathe to calm his anger, but when I asked him to show me how he did this, he took a huge, rapid in-breath that would effectively activate instead of calm him. By asking him to show me what he knew, I learned that I needed to start with helping him refine his breathing technique.

PROCESSING: Ask clients what mindfulness skills they have practiced before and how they felt about them. Use the information you gain from this tool to know where to start with this client and to know what objections clients may have.

Tool 4-10: Find Out How Client is Already Being Mindful

THEORY: Most people are mindful already in some part of their day, whether they realize it or not. Helping them to notice and identify times when they are being mindful helps them to embrace the process and aids in increasing their self-awareness. It also provides more information about where they are in the process of incorporating mindfulness. This tool explains how to help clients identify when they are being mindful.

IMPLEMENTATION: Explain what being mindful is using the definition in Tools 2-1 through 2-3. Tell clients that mindfulness is being fully present, paying attention to what they are doing or to something in particular. Ask the client to think about their day and identify when they were being mindful. Give them some suggestions about when they might have been. Were they fully present and mindful when they were talking to their spouse or child? Did their mindfulness increase when they tripped or avoided an accident? Were they mindful when they tasted the food they were cooking? What were they thinking about when they chose what to wear today? Were they mindful when they took a shower, drove to work, smelled the fresh-cut grass, listened to their favorite song on the radio, answered the phone, or looked at Facebook posts? If they can't think of any time they were mindful, ask them what they did today and go over it with them. Help them find at least one time when they were probably being mindful. Let them know they are being mindful right now while they are doing this exercise.

PROCESSING: Everyone is mindful sometimes. Explain what being mindful is and help your client identify times when they were being mindful. Help them understand mindfulness and discuss what caused them to be mindful. Discuss why being mindful is helpful and important.

Tool 4-11: How to Start Small and Where the Client is

THEORY: As always, in any helping profession, we must start where the client is. Use Tool 4-10 to determine where the client is. This tool uses the information gleaned from Tool 4-10 to decide what mindfulness skills to start with.

IMPLEMENTATION: No matter what you have determined that the client already knows about mindfulness, it is helpful to review their knowledge and make sure it is accurate. After doing so, you can decide what mindfulness skills to teach first. Since breathing and awareness of breath are such staples of mindfulness, this is often a great place to start. Don't expect a mindfulness newbie to start right in with a 15- or 20- minute sitting meditation, especially if they have trouble sitting still, as might those with ADHD or anxiety.

To begin, the Awareness of Breath Tool (Tool 5-5) might be used ending with a brief period of silence and gradually increasing it as the client practices and gains more skill. Depending on their previous experience and what else you know about them, you might start with an Awareness of Surroundings exercise (Tools 6-1 through 6-5), which is easy to do, only takes a few minutes, can be done anywhere, is usually very relaxing, demonstrates mindfulness, and is generally non-threatening to the client.

On the other hand, if they are more experienced, you might review the basics and start with an Awareness of Thoughts or Emotions (Chapters 7 and 8). For more advanced clients a more formal sitting meditation may be a good option. Take into consideration the issues the client is dealing with in choosing the specific skills that may be most helpful to them. See Tools 2-21 and 4-12.

PROCESSING: Gather as much information as possible about what this client needs help with and what their experience level is with mindfulness. Use this knowledge to decide which mindfulness skills to start with. A good progression might be belly breathing, awareness of breath, present moment and surroundings, intentions, tasks, physical body, thoughts, emotions, relationships, and compassion for self and others. This progression will vary depending on the needs and experience of the client.

Tool 4-12: Choose the Best Mindfulness Skill(s) for the Client

THEORY: Each client will embrace different mindfulness skills that suit them the best. Some will prefer a guided meditation. Others will succeed in doing a sitting meditation on their own. Some will incorporate mindfulness throughout their day while others may prefer a more formal sitting practice. Some will be partial to sitting still while others may prefer a walking or movement meditation. This tool explains how to help clients choose mindfulness skills that they enjoy, and from which they receive the most benefit.

IMPLEMENTATION: This first step in this tool is to get to know your client. Find out about their previous experience with mindfulness, how they might benefit from the practice, and what issues they are dealing with. For example, if a client has the symptoms of poor concentration and hyperactivity associated with ADHD, then begin with briefer meditations and those that include movement. Clients with ADHD may be put off if you start by asking them to sit still for more than a minute or two as sitting still is exactly what they may be having difficulty doing. Doing so may cause them to reject the whole practice of mindfulness. If they start with a 30-second silent period and master that, then they can gradually increase the period by

30 seconds until at some point they can sit for 5 or 10 minutes. Belly breathing (Tool 5-2) and a movement meditation such as walking (Tools 15-1 through 15-4) or an Awareness of Tasks (Tools 11-1 and 11-2) practice may be just right for someone with ADHD.

If the client is highly anxious, a long meditation of inner reflection may initially be too anxiety provoking for them. Teach them breathing techniques to help them learn to calm their physiology as well as more active mindfulness skills such as Awareness of Surroundings (Tools 6-1 through 6-5) and Awareness of Tasks (Tools 11-1 and 11-2). As they become more comfortable, add in brief Awareness of Physical Body (Tools 9-1 through 9-4) and eventually Awareness of Thoughts (Tools 7-1 through 7-5) and Awareness of Emotions (Tools 8-1 through 8-3) skills.

Keeping an open dialogue with your client about what their experience is like as they do each mindfulness skill will provide you with the information you need to modify skill choices or fine-tune existing choices.

If a client doesn't like a particular mindfulness skill for whatever reason, don't give up. Ask them why they don't like it, make sure they are doing it in such a way that it should benefit them, modify it, or choose a different skill.

PROCESSING: Learn as much as possible about your client and their needs. Select and review mindfulness skills you think will help them. Discuss a variety of mindfulness skills with them and engage them to be part of the solution by making choices about with skills they will try. This is possible and helpful with individuals as well as group participants. Check in with your client about how their practice is going, modify current choices, and add more appropriate skills as needed.

TOOLS FOR RELATING EFFECTIVENESS OF SPECIFIC SKILLS TO THEIR CONDITION

Tool 4-13: Relate Benefits to the Client's Condition

THEORY: Most clients want to know how practicing mindfulness might help them. Giving them information about the studies on the effectiveness of mindfulness for their particular issues will make them more likely to invest in their own practice. Sharing anecdotal clinical results also helps the client relate mindfulness practice to their own specific issues/conditions. This tool explains how to help the client make the connection between potential personal benefits and mindfulness practice.

IMPLEMENTATION: Learn as much as possible about your client and the issues/conditions they present with. Explain how mindfulness practice might improve their conditions. Tell them about specific studies that have shown an improvement in conditions like theirs. See Tools 2-20 and 2-21 for more information about the studies. In general, studies have shown improvements in depression, anxiety, sleep, concentration, hyperactivity, anger, sense of well-being, quality of life, chronic illness, pain, rumination, stress, hope, joy, long-term mental health, binge eating, compassion, fibromyalgia, rheumatoid arthritis, immunity, substance use, and more. Tell them how mindfulness changes the brain and why it works for their condition.

Chances are good that you can find a study that relates the benefits of mindfulness practice to the condition(s) your client has. Even if no studies show a direct correlation, you may help them make the connection. For example, if they suffer from a painful loss of a loved one, mindfulness practice won't bring back the loved one, but it can help with the sadness, worry, and sense of well-being. With time you will accrue many examples from your own practice of clients whose conditions improved with mindfulness practice, which you can share with current clients (of course, protecting confidentiality). If appropriate with this client, you might also share your personal story of how mindfulness has helped you. You are practicing yourself, right?

PROCESSING: After explaining the benefits to your client, make sure they understand why mindfulness practice might help them. Ask them to explain in their own words what benefits they expect. Answer any questions they may have.

Tool 4-14: Journal About Benefits You Expect from Mindfulness

THEORY: Clients will become more invested in starting a mindfulness practice if they can relate the potential benefits to their own personal issues or conditions. This tool provides journal prompts to help clients reflect on what mindfulness might help them with and what benefits they expect.

IMPLEMENTATION: Ask the client to reply to the journal prompts in Handout 4-14. Explain that doing so will help them clarify what they've learned about how mindfulness practice might help them with their issues/conditions. It will also help them define what benefits they hope to gain from their practice.

PROCESSING: Review your client's answers to the journal prompts. Use this process as a springboard for discussion about the benefits of mindfulness. Connect the benefits to your client's particular issues/conditions. Ask them if they feel comfortable making a commitment to mindfulness practice in order to help with a specific condition or even simply to gain an improved sense of well-being.

HANDOUT 4-14
JOURNAL ABOUT BENEFITS YOU EXPECT FROM MINDFULNESS

Journal Prompts:

- What benefits do studies show can be achieved through mindfulness practice?
- Do any of these benefits relate to issues or conditions you experience?
- What surprised you most about the research?
- What personal issues/conditions would you like to improve?
- How might mindfulness practice be helpful to you?
- Are you skeptical about the benefits?
- Do you think mindfulness practice will help you?
- Are you willing and able to make a commitment to incorporating mindfulness practice into your life on a regular basis?
- Are the potential benefits reason enough for you to give mindfulness a try?
- What reservations do you have about practicing mindfulness?
- If mindfulness practice could help you with just one thing, what would you want that to be?
- Would you be willing to practice mindfulness if it simply increased your sense of well-being?
- What emotion arises when you consider how mindfulness practice might help you?

Section III

TOOLS FOR TEACHING SPECIFIC MINDFULNESS SKILLS

Chapter 5: Mindfulness of Breath

Tool 5-1: Basic Relaxation Breathing

THEORY: By changing our breathing pattern we indirectly change our physiology. When we breathe in, or inhale, we activate our sympathetic nervous system, which activates our physiology as well as our stress response. This is often called the fight or flight response. When we activate our sympathetic nervous system, our heart rate increases, pupils dilate, blood vessels constrict, sweat increases, and the digestive system slows down. We get more alert and overall tension increases.

When we breathe out, or exhale, we activate our parasympathetic nervous system. The parasympathetic nervous system is responsible for the "rest and digest" activities that occur when the body is at rest. Therefore, when we exhale, our heart rate slows down, intestinal and glandular activity increases, and we generally feel more relaxed.

The practice of focusing on our breathing leads to reflective rather than reactive responses. It gives us control over our responses so we respond rather than react.

IMPLEMENTATION: Explain that inhaling activates the sympathetic nervous system and exhaling activates the parasympathetic nervous system. Use Handout 5-1 to explain the relaxation breathing technique. Demonstrate the technique and do it with clients.

PROCESSING: This breathing technique very quickly calms the physiology of the body and brain. Most clients feel calmer and less anxious within two to three breaths. This is a great place to start most mindfulness exercises and is the basis for the core practice. By practicing this breathing technique, you will effectively lower your stress response and improve your physical, emotional, and cognitive health. Caution clients to inhale slowly while counting to four instead of taking a rapid inhale, which may increase the stress response instead of calming it down.

HANDOUT 5-1
BASIC RELAXATION BREATHING

A breathing technique that is very helpful in deactivating the stress response consists of breathing in through the nose to the count of four and breathing out through the mouth to the count of eight. Thus, we activate the parasympathetic nervous system twice as long as the sympathetic nervous system with a net result of calming our physiology and stress response.

Try this simple technique as often as you think of it. Breathe in through your nose to the count of four and out through your mouth to the count of eight. When you exhale, purse your lips and blow gently like you are blowing out a candle or blowing a bubble. This will help you slow down the exhale. Don't worry if your nose is stuffy, just breathe in and out through your mouth instead.

Inhale through your nose: 1-2-3-4.

Exhale through your mouth with lips pursed, blowing gently, like blowing a bubble: 1-2-3-4-5-6-7-8.

Repeat 3–4 times.

Practice this breathing technique often throughout the day. You might choose to take a nice slow breath every time you answer the phone, when you get into the car, when you visit the bathroom, before you eat, and certainly if you are feeling stressed. Pick a few times that work best for you to help you get in the habit of doing one to three deep breaths in through your nose to the count of four and out through your mouth to the count of eight.

Tool 5-2: How to Belly Breathe

THEORY: Deep breathing, or diaphragmatic breathing, is often referred to as "Belly Breathing." It involves inhaling and filling the lungs in such a way as to expand the stomach, not the chest. In belly breathing the lungs expand downward, allowing much more air to be inhaled than during a chest breath. A chest breath is the same as anxious breathing while a belly breath is considered to be relaxation breathing. It provides much more oxygen to the body and helps to lower the stress response.

IMPLEMENTATION: Use Handout 5-2 to teach clients how to belly breathe. Demonstrate it and do it with them.

PROCESSING: Belly breathing can be totally new to many clients. Some may have learned it if they took yoga or singing classes, but most have not. Most adults try to hold in their stomachs to prevent the appearance of a pot belly, which can limit the ability to get a deep belly breath. Demonstrate doing a belly breath for them. See Tool 5-3 for how to know if they are getting a belly breath. It may be helpful for the client to lie on their back to get the feel of a belly breath. Have them practice at least several times a day. It can be combined with the Basic Relaxation Breathing Tool 5-1.

HANDOUT 5-2
HOW TO BELLY BREATHE

1. Place one hand on your abdomen above your belly button and one hand on your upper chest.

2. Relax your abdomen.

3. Breathe in through your nose and fill your lungs.

4. Allow your lungs to expand downward and move the bottom hand.

5. Avoid shallow chest breathing or raising your shoulders.

6. Exhale slowly through pursed lips.

Tool 5-3: Three Ways to Tell if You are Belly Breathing

THEORY: Belly breathing has been shown to be an important part of decreasing the stress response. It increases the oxygen intake and generally increases awareness of breathing, which is a basic concept in mindfulness.

IMPLEMENTATION: Use Handout 5-3 to teach clients how to know if they are getting a belly breath. Explain and demonstrate these three techniques and watch clients try each of them in session. Encourage them to practice several times a day between sessions until they can readily tell they are belly breathing.

PROCESSING: Learning to belly breathe takes practice for most clients. These three easy ways to tell if you are getting a belly breath help clients gain mastery over this technique very quickly. Explain and demonstrate the three techniques, do them with clients, and then follow up at subsequent sessions by asking them to show you how they are doing with them.

HANDOUT 5-3
THREE WAYS TO TELL IF YOU ARE BELLY BREATHING

There are three easy ways to tell if you are belly breathing or chest breathing.

1. Place one hand on your abdomen above your belly button and one hand on your upper chest. Just breathe as you usually breathe and notice which hand moves more. If the bottom hand moves more, great, that's a belly breath. If the top hand moves more, that's a chest breath, which is the same as anxious breathing. Deliberately move your stomach in and out just below your rib cage and above your belly button to get the feel of a belly breathe. Notice when you breathe normally which hand moves more.

   Bottom hand moves more = belly breath—great
   Top hand moves more—chest breath = same as anxious breathing

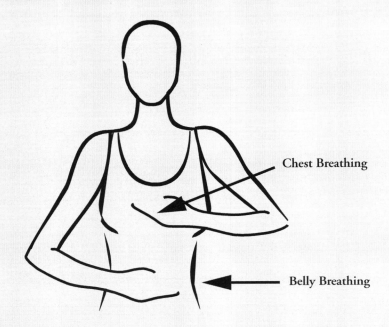

Chest Breathing

Belly Breathing

2. **Intentionally take a chest breath and blow on your hand.** Notice the temperature of the air as it flows across your fingers. Now, intentionally take a belly breath and blow on your hand. Again, notice the temperature of the air as it flows across your fingers. You will notice that the air feels warmer when it comes from a belly breath.

Chest breath $\rightarrow$ colder air
Belly breath $\rightarrow$ warmer air

3. **Lie down on your back.** Place an object on your belly such as a book or pillow. For children, you might use a small stuffed animal. Now make the object go up and down as you breathe.

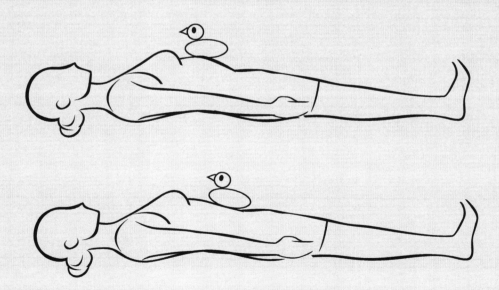

Tool 5-4: Core Practice

THEORY: At the heart of mindfulness is the Core Practice. Core Practice is a way to tell our minds to relax and focus and to calm down the "monkey brain." It can be used several times a day, almost like pushing the reset button. It is the perfect way to remind ourselves to be mindful.

IMPLEMENTATION: Use Handout 5-4 to teach clients the basics of Core Practice. Modify the length of the silent period to suit the needs of the client and lengthen it as they practice and gain mastery. This might range from 10 seconds for a beginner or hyperactive or anxious client, on up to 15 minutes for a more advanced client.

PROCESSING: Teach the client to reflect on the process of breathing. Ask them what the practice was like for them; how they felt as they breathed; what they noticed about their breathing; how they stayed focused on breathing; and what they did when their mind wandered. Normalize their experience—it is normal for the mind to wander. Recommend they practice this several times a day. They may eventually use a short version of the practice (5 or 10 seconds) and incorporate it into their day to center or ground themselves during transitions or before starting an activity.

HANDOUT 5-4
CORE PRACTICE

PAUSE → LISTEN → BREATHE

Find yourself a comfortable position.

Close your eyes.

Pay attention to your breathing.

Breathe slowly in through your nose and out through your mouth.

Imagine the air slowly filling your lungs and body and then flowing out again.

When you notice that your mind has wandered, acknowledge it, accept it, and then bring your attention back to your breath.

Notice your belly moving as you take slow belly breaths.

Continue for a minute (Note: shorten or lengthen as needed).

Open your eyes and return to the room.

Tool 5-5: Awareness of Breath Meditation

THEORY: The Awareness of Breath Meditation is a guided meditation that leads clients through the process of paying attention to their breathing in every detail. It helps them get in touch with the feel of their breath and helps them practice the process of noticing when their mind wanders and bringing their attention back to their breath. This meditation improves focus and mental clarity, calms the anxious brain, and improves self-regulation.

IMPLEMENTATION: Handout 5-5 contains an Awareness of Breath Meditation. Explain to clients that this meditation involves paying attention to the breath and will help them relax, concentrate, and improve their self-awareness and their sense of well-being. Explain that it is normal for thoughts to wander and that when they notice they are thinking about something other than their breath, they can acknowledge it, dismiss it, and gently bring their attention back to their breath.

You may read the text of this meditation to your client in session. It will take a little more than 5 minutes to do it. Ask them to find a comfortable position either sitting upright in a chair with arms and leg uncrossed, or lying down with arms and legs uncrossed, or if they are comfortable in a cross-legged position, sitting on the floor or cushion with legs crossed. Suggest that they place their hands palms up on their thighs with their thumb and middle finger touching.

PROCESSING: At the end of the meditation allow a moment for the client to open their eyes and reorient themselves to the room. Then help the client reflect on what they experienced during the Awareness of Breath Meditation. You might ask them how they felt while they were doing the meditation. Did they notice any sensations in their body? Did any particular thoughts arise? How did they handle distracting thoughts? Do they feel any different after the meditation than before doing it? Did they experience any difficulty? What did they like about it? Normalize wandering thoughts. Tell them practice makes perfect. Emphasize there is no one right way to do this.

HANDOUT 5-5
AWARENESS OF BREATH MEDITATION

Let's begin with a breathing technique that involves breathing in through your nose to the count of four and exhaling through your mouth to the count of eight. Let's start by taking a deep belly breath in through your nose to the count of four. 1-2-3-4. Now slowly breathe out to the count of eight, pursing your lips as if you were gently blowing out a candle or blowing a bubble. 1-2-3-4-5-6-7-8. Do it again. Inhale through your nose to the count of four (1-2-3-4) and exhale through your mouth to the count of eight (1-2-3-4-5-6-7-8).

Now just breathe normally. As you do this, notice how the air feels as it comes into your body. You might notice the feeling of the breath as it flows into your nose. Pay attention to it. Is the air cool, warm, or perhaps neutral? Does it feel silky, soft, or hard? Is there an odor or fragrance? Follow it and notice how it feels as it flows past your nostrils, up into your nasal passageways, and down the back of your throat. Notice the sensations as the air fills your lungs from the bottom, gradually filling them up to the top. Be aware of the air as you exhale. Empty your lungs starting at the top and going gradually down to the bottom. Is the air warmer as it comes up into your throat when exhaling? Observe how it feels when the air flows up your throat, into your mouth, across your lips. Keep noticing your breath as it flows in and out of you. Send your affection and caring to this wonderful breath, as it flows down into your lungs and then back out again. Allow it to flow as it brings the life force into your being. Enjoy the feeling of nourishment and healing as you continue to breathe in and then out.

Do you notice any change in your breathing now that you have been paying attention to it? Is your breathing deep, shallow? Are you breathing slowly, rapidly, gently, sharply? Observe your breathing pattern without changing it. Become aware of the peace and warmth and healing that breathing brings to your being. Allow it. Accept it. Own it. It is yours and yours alone. Allow your breath to fill every part of your body. Let it bring comfort and healing wherever it's needed. Take an intentional breath in and breathe in peace and healing. Now exhale and allow anything that needs to go to flow effortlessly out. Allow your breath to cleanse and heal. Observe it. Be with it. If your mind wanders, that's ok, accept it; every mind wanders while doing this. Just bring your attention back to your breath. Send loving thoughts to your breath.

Be in touch with feelings of gratitude—be thankful for the breath that so effortlessly gives you life. Marvel at the wonder of breathing. Isn't it amazing how your body breathes automatically far beneath conscious thought? Appreciate how your body just knows what to do with this precious breath of air without any thinking or doing on your part. Just being.

Take another intentional breath in through your nose to the count of four. 1-2-3-4. Now exhale through your mouth to the count of eight. 1-2-3-4-5-6-7-8. Do it again. Inhale peace, relaxation, harmony. Exhale and observe that what needs to go is going on its own. Now breathe normally again. Float on the cushion of your own breath. Breathing is effortless. Enjoy and appreciate the wonderful phenomenon of breathing.

Now bring your awareness back to the room when you are ready.

Spend a few minutes reflecting on what came up during the meditation.

Tool 5-6: Counting Sets of Four Breaths

THEORY: Counting sets of four breaths is a simple mindfulness practice that anyone can do. Even young clients who can count to four have enjoyed seeing how many sets of breaths they can count. The tool teaches mindfulness, focus, present moment awareness, and letting go of distractions. This practice can be quite calming as well as fun.

IMPLEMENTATION: Use Handout 5-6 to teach the client how to do this mindfulness skill. Discuss the benefit of practicing this skill. Explain that this is a fun, playful way to see how long they can focus on counting breaths before they notice they have stopped counting.

PROCESSING: Ask clients to reflect on what happened for them while doing this. Were they able to stay focused? How many sets were they able to count to? Clients often have fun doing this and they like to make a game out of seeing how many sets they count before forgetting to count, sometimes competing with a friend. It can be done while walking or working out, or doing crafts such as knitting. Some clients have reported practicing it while they are driving!

HANDOUT 5-6
COUNTING SETS OF FOUR BREATHS

Close your eyes and take a deep belly breath in through your nose to the count of four and then exhale slowly through your mouth with pursed lips to the count of eight like blowing a bubble. (Do this with your client a couple of times.)

Then breathe normally while observing the feeling of the breath. Now start counting each exhale. When you have counted four exhales, hold one finger out and count that as one set of four. Continue counting another four exhales and hold out a second finger, thereby counting a second set of four. Continue to do this for several minutes.

Every time you notice that your attention has wandered from counting your breaths and you have started to focus on some other thought or feeling, simply accept it, dismiss it, and return your attention to counting your exhales.

See how many sets of four exhales you can count on your fingers before you realize you have stopped counting. For beginners 10 sets is a lot.

Tool 5-7: Journal About Breathing

THEORY: Journaling can be an effective way for clients to process and integrate their experiences while learning mindfulness. Some clients will love to journal. Others will not. If a client is not comfortable writing, ask them to draw a picture that represents something about their experience with mindfulness of breathing. If they don't want to journal, you might still ask them the following prompts and process their verbal responses.

IMPLEMENTATION: Ask the client to respond to the journal prompts in Handout 5-7 about how the breathing exercises in this entire chapter have affected their life.

PROCESSING: Ask your client if they want to share their journal entries with you. Discuss what they write. Normalize any difficulty they are having with focusing or being self-critical about learning mindfulness. Help them process the feelings that they express during this process.

HANDOUT 5-7
JOURNAL ABOUT BREATHING

Journal Prompts:

- What happened when you practiced breathing meditations?
- What thoughts, feelings, and sensations arose?
- How did you feel when you focused on breathing?
- What did you notice about your breathing?
- Did you notice your mind wandering?
- How did you bring your attention back to breathing?
- When have you used the mindfulness of breathing skills?
- When could you have used them?
- How has practicing these breathing exercises changed your day?
- What did you like most about breathing exercises?
- What did you like least about breathing exercises?
- Have you noticed any changes in your stress level?
- Have you noticed any changes in your ability to concentrate?
- Has anything changed for you?

Chapter 6: Present Moment Awareness

MINDFULNESS OF SURROUNDINGS

Tool 6-1: Mindfulness of Surroundings—Indoors

THEORY: One basic component of being aware in the present moment is being aware of the immediate surroundings. This mindfulness tool teaches the skill of being totally present in this moment while focusing on all the details of the surroundings. It uses as many of the senses as possible for an integrated awareness. Starting with the surroundings is a safe and comfortable place to begin teaching present moment awareness as it tends to be less threatening and personal than inner awareness exercises.

IMPLEMENTATION: Explain that this brief mindfulness meditation teaches the ability to stay totally present in this moment. Note to clients that although you will be asking questions, you don't want a verbal response. Explain that clients should just listen to the questions and answer them in their head as they explore their surroundings.

Read Handout 6-1 aloud to lead the listener through a guided awareness of surroundings meditation. Encourage them to practice a brief version of this skill when they first arrive in new surroundings such as when getting to work, school, a store, or perhaps onto a highway to help them transition and bring their focus to their present surroundings.

PROCESSING: Ask your client what happened for them during the meditation. Ask them: What did you notice? Did you notice anything new? How did your body feel? What was going on in your mind? Were you distracted and if so, by what? What did you do to stay focused?

HANDOUT 6-1
PRESENT MOMENT AWARENESS

MINDFULNESS OF SURROUNDINGS

Find yourself a comfortable position in your chair with feet flat on the floor, back resting gently against the back of the chair, thumb and middle finger connected in a loop, and hands resting gently palms up on your thighs. Keep your eyes open and focused on your surroundings whether you are inside a room or outside in nature.

Look around. Pay attention to what you see. Is it bright or dark? Are you alone or with others? Are you inside or outside? If you are inside, are there windows in the room? Can you see outside? Can you see the sky? Is there light, or sunshine shining in the window? Does it light up an area on the floor or the wall? If you are outside, can you see the sky? Are there clouds? Is the sun shining?

What is straight ahead of you? What is beside you? Can you see behind you? Look all the way around you. Observe. When your mind wanders, notice it, accept it, and then bring your attention back to looking around you again.

Notice the temperature around you. Is it warm, cold, just right? Is the air moving or still? Do you smell any odors or smells? Are they comforting or distasteful? Are they new smells or are they familiar?

What can you hear? Is it quiet? Is there noise? What sounds are there? Where are they coming from? Are they loud, soft, sharp, soothing, or annoying? Do you want to keep listening to the sounds or do you want them to stop?

Is there activity in the space? What is moving? What stays still? Are things moving through the space, coming and going?

Pay attention to your body sitting in the chair. Feel where your bottom is supported by the chair. Is the chair hard, soft, cushiony, or solid? Is the back supporting your back? Does the chair fit you? Do your feet touch the floor or swing above it? Do your knees bend at the edge of the chair? Do you fill the seat side to side?

Look around and find something that particularly attracts your attention. Notice what shape it is, where it is located, what color it is, its texture, its purpose. Observe why it draws your attention. Does it remind you of something else? Do you know what it is? Is it common, or unusual? When thoughts arise that are not about this present moment, notice them, accept them, and let them go. Tell them "not now." Bring your awareness back to your surroundings.

Become aware of yourself in this space. How do you feel? Do you feel safe? Do you want to be here? Does this place feel familiar or does everything seem new to you? Have you been someplace else that reminds you of this place? Do you feel good, bad, or neutral here?

Notice the energy you feel in this place. Become aware of your inner reaction to being in this place. Is it active or quiet energy? Is it calm, bubbling, hot, cold? Is it positive, negative? Is it peaceful or bustling? Is it intense or mild? Is it toxic here? Or healing?

Now that you have spent some time completely focused on being in this moment, bring the awareness you have gained back with you as you resume your regular life. Practice this exercise whenever possible to keep yourself present in the moment. You will increase your concentration, productivity, and lower your stress response.

Tool 6-2: Mindfulness Outside in Nature

THEORY: Being aware of the present moment is one central aspect of mindfulness. This mindfulness tool teaches the skill of being totally present in this moment while focusing on all the details of natural surroundings. It uses as many of the senses as possible for an integrated awareness. This tool incorporates awareness of surroundings with the well-known healing, calming effect of being outside in nature.

IMPLEMENTATION: Explain that this tool is an excellent way to improve present moment awareness. Ask your client to close their eyes and use their imagination as you read the Mindfulness in Nature Meditation in Handout 6-2. Explain that they can do this process any time they are outdoors and recommend that they do it for a minute or two each time they go outside.

PROCESSING: After reading the meditation, ask your client what it was like for them to pay such close attention to the nature around them. Were they able to use their imagination to pretend they were outside? Was it difficult to stay focused? What distracted them? How did they bring their attention back to the present moment? Were they able to practice it themselves during the week when they were actually outside? What did they notice when they did it? How did they feel before, during, and after the exercise?

HANDOUT 6-2
MINDFULNESS IN NATURE MEDITATION

Practice this skill every time you are outside, whether it's to go for a walk, to sit on the deck, or even when you are walking to your car.

Whenever you are outside, practice being in the present moment. Notice your surroundings.

Start by looking at the sky. What color is it right now? Is it clear? Are there clouds? What do the clouds look like? Is the sun shining? Is it behind the clouds? Is it daylight or after dark?

Look around and see what's around you. Can you see some trees? If so, look closely at one of the trees. Is it covered with leaves or are the branches bare? What color are the leaves or the branches? Are there buds on the branches or seed pods or flowers? Does it have needles and pine cones? Is the tree perfectly still or is it moving in the breeze?

Slowly inhale and notice what you smell. Is there a fragrance or odor? Is it pleasant or distasteful? Is it natural or man-made? Does it remind you of something or of another time in your life?

Can you see grass? What color is it? Is it lush and green or dried out and brittle? Is it long or nicely groomed? If you can, reach down and touch the grass. What does it feel like?

Are there any flowers blooming? Notice their colors and shapes. Smell them if you can.

Are there any rocks in view? Look at their shape and color. Touch them and notice their texture.

Can you see a lake or the ocean? Pay attention to the water. Is it calm and still or moving and full of waves? What color is the water? Is there a beach?

Listen. What do you hear? Are there birds singing? Do you hear the sounds of civilization such as cars, trucks, planes, motors, horns, sirens? Can you hear the breeze blowing in the trees? Is there a sound from a stream or a waterfall or ocean surf?

Pay attention to the temperature. Is it hot, cold, warm, or chilly? Is the air still or is there a breeze, or perhaps a stiff wind?

Now that you have spent some time focusing completely on your natural surroundings, bring your heightened awareness with you as you resume your daily activities.

AWARENESS OF OBJECT

Tool 6-3: Beginner's Mind with Any Object

THEORY: To see the richness of the present moment, we need to cultivate what has been called "beginner's mind." According to Jon Kabat-Zinn, beginner's mind is a mind that is willing to see everything as if for the first time. This tool is a present moment awareness exercise that uses awareness of any object to practice using beginner's mind to see the object as if for the first time.

IMPLEMENTATION: Explain to your client that two of the basics of mindfulness are beginner's mind and present moment awareness. Explain that this exercise helps them use beginner's mind, which is a mind that is open and willing to see everything as if for the first time, as they practice present moment awareness.

Use the process described in Handout 6-3 with any object that is small enough to be held. Some examples of objects to use include a pencil, an eraser, a piece of paper, a cup, a fork, a ball, a toy. Use whatever you have handy. Hold the same type of object yourself and follow the instructions as you lead the exercise.

PROCESSING: Ask the client what happened for them while they did this exercise. Did they notice anything about the object they hadn't noticed before? Were they able to stay focused? Was it boring? Did they notice any change in how they were feeling as they focused on the object?

Choose an object that is small enough to pick up easily and hold in your hand. Hold it in one hand and pass it to the other hand. Notice how heavy or light it is in your hand. How big is it? Rub your fingers over the surface. Are the edges rough or smooth? Observe the shape, color, and texture of the object. Feel any imperfections in the surface or ridges or indentations. Pay attention to whether it feels smooth, or rough. Does it feel cool or warm to your fingers? Is it sticky, greasy, slippery, wet, or dry?

Look closely to see if there is anything written on it. Are there words on it? Are there designs drawn or printed on it? If your mind wanders or you start thinking about how bored you are, just bring your awareness back to the object. Squeeze it between your fingers. Is it squishy, flexible, hard, or solid?

How does it sound when you tap on it with your finger or scrape it with your fingernail? Does it echo, thud, click, thump, rattle? Rotate it in your hand. How does the light reflect off it? Is it shiny or dull? Does it reflect light, like a mirror? Is the color solid, opaque, transparent? Can you see through it? Is it solid or hollow? What material is it made out of?

Hold it up to your nose and smell it. Does it have an odor? Is it stinky or fragrant or neutral? Can you drop it on the table? Does it stay still or roll around or teeter in place? What sound does it make as you move it around the table? Does it slide easily or stick in one place? Look closely and find something you didn't notice before.

Tool 6-4: Water Glass

THEORY: This tool is another present moment awareness skill using a glass of water as the object to observe. Using water allows the client to engage the sense of sight, touch, smell, taste, and hearing. This tool gives an excellent example of engaging "beginner's mind" to observe the glass of water.

IMPLEMENTATION: Explain to clients that you will lead them in a present moment awareness exercise using a glass of water as the object of their attention. Use Handout 6-4 as a guideline. After you have read through the handout yourself and understand the concept, put it down and hold a glass (or cup) of water in your own hand and do the exercise yourself as you lead the meditation. Ask the client to open their mind and look at the glass of water like they've never seen one before.

PROCESSING: Ask the client what this was like for them. Did they notice anything in particular about the glass? How did it feel to pay attention to the glass and then the water? What did they notice about the taste or the smell? Were they able to follow the water as it went down their throat? How did they handle distracting thoughts? Do they feel any different now compared to before the exercise?

HANDOUT 6-4
PRESENT MOMENT AWARENESS: WATER GLASS

Fill a glass (or cup) half full of water. Look at the glass as it sits on the table. Notice the shape, color, and size. Pick up the glass and look at it from all sides. Is there anything written on the sides or bottom? Rub your fingers across each surface of the glass. Is it smooth, rough, sticky, slippery? Is it curved or squared? Are there any rough edges?

Can you see through the glass? Move the glass back and forth and notice what happens to the water inside. Does it move? Move the glass in circles and watch the water swirl around the edges of the glass. Now hold it still. What happens to the water?

Tap on the glass below the water line. What does it sound like? Now tap on the glass above the water line. Does the sound change? Tap on the bottom and then on the rim. How does the sound differ?

Bring the glass up toward your nose and sniff it. Is there any odor? Is it pleasant, unpleasant, familiar, or perhaps surprising?

Take a small sip of water and hold it in your mouth. What does wet feel like? Is it hot, cold, silky, or rough? What does it feel like as you move it around your mouth? Swallow.

Take another sip and notice how the water feels as it comes into your mouth. Swallow it and pay attention to how it feels as it flows down your throat and into your stomach. Where do you lose track of it?

Bring your awareness back to the room.

OPEN FOCUS

Tool 6-5: Can You Imagine the Space Between?

THEORY: Open Focus was developed by Les Fehmi (Fehmi, 2007, 2010, 2012). Its practice helps to develop attentional skills, the most basic skill in mindfulness. Open Focus attention training encourages awareness of how you attend to the wide array of sensory experiences, and the space between those experiences. It helps you put things in perspective and helps to relieve stress, manage physical pain, regulate emotions, and set the stage for peak performance and transcendent moments. For more information, see *The Open Focus Brain*: *Harnessing the Power of Attention to Heal Mind and Body* (Fehmi, 2007*)*.

IMPLEMENTATION: Explain that Open Focus is a present moment awareness tool that trains diffuse versus narrow attention in the present moment. It is designed to help clients put things in perspective. For example, when they feel depressed for a day, to put it in perspective and remember that they have felt better and will again soon. One day is not everything and is less significant in the context of a whole year. Ask clients to find a comfortable position and close their eyes if they feel comfortable. Then read through the Open Focus meditation (Handout 6-5).

PROCESSING: Ask your client what this experience was like for them. Were they able to visualize the space "between"? Did they notice any change in their physiological arousal state? Do they feel more relaxed now? What did they like/dislike about this exercise? Were they able to stay focused? Did they notice the difference between large and small spaces?

HANDOUT 6-5
OPEN FOCUS: CAN YOU IMAGINE THE SPACE BETWEEN?

Bring all your awareness to the space between your eyes.
Get a feeling of the space.
Visualize the space.
Hear the silence between the eyes.
Think about the space.
Have a sense of newness between the eyes.
After seeing it, imagine feeling the space.

Put your thumbs together.
Can you imagine the space between the thumbs?
Can you imagine the shape?
Imagine what's around the thumbs.
Imagine what's outside the thumbs.
Feel nothing—absence of thumbs.
Can you feel the space around the thumbs?
Can you feel the sense of presence on your thumbs and index fingers?
Can you feel the space between the fingers and thumbs?
More of the brain's cortex is devoted to your awareness of this area of your body than any other part of the body.
Can you imagine feeling the space between the other fingers as well?
Can you imagine that throughout this exercise you will use this example of space to imagine what other spaces
feel like during the exercise?

Effortlessly allow your imagination do all the work.
You will try to consciously grip the space which is not grippable.
You will focus more on how you are paying attention to it.
It occurs on an unconscious level.
You will release a lot of tension.

You will loosen and your focus will open.
When you are open you diffuse stress and tension.
When you are not open you accumulate tension.
If an unpleasant feeling occurs it is just a small thing in the totality of your total focus.
This practice builds a kind of refuge that helps you deal with things.
This provides a way for normalizing physiology.
Sit gently erect to avoid dropping out or sleeping.

(Adapted with permission from www.openfocus.com) (Fehmi, 2007, 2007, 2010)

Can you imagine the space inside your head?
Can you imagine the space between the top of your head and the bottom of your feet?
Can you imagine the space between your left ear and right ear?
Can you imagine the space between your shoulders and your toes?
Can you imagine the space inside your mouth?

Can you imagine the space between your back and the back of the chair?
Can you imagine the space between your fingers?
Can you imagine the space between your shoulders and your hips?
Can you imagine the space between your mouth and your nose?
Can you imagine the space between your hips and your toes?
Can you imagine the space between your ankles and your heels?
Bring your focus back to the room.

JOURNAL

Tool 6-7: Journal About How Present Moment Awareness Changes My Day

THEORY: Journaling will help the client consolidate what they have learned about present moment awareness as well as point out where they may need more guidance.

IMPLEMENTATION: Ask the client to respond to the journal prompts listed in Handout 6-7. Explain that this is an excellent way for them to consolidate and integrate what they have learned and also to identify where they need more practice.

PROCESSING: Review the client's answers to the journal prompts with them. Use this as a springboard for discussion about what they've learned and what they still need help with.

HANDOUT 6-7
JOURNAL ABOUT HOW PRESENT MOMENT AWARENESS CHANGES MY DAY

Journal Prompts:

- Describe what Present Moment Awareness (PMA) is.
- Give some examples of when you practiced this.
- How can you practice PMA while answering these prompts?
- How has your ability to be aware in the present moment changed?
- What have you noticed about your body when you practice this skill?
- What have you noticed about your emotional state when you practice this skill?
- When might you have practiced this skill that you didn't?
- How has your life changed now that you practice present moment awareness?
- How have you practiced using "beginner's mind"?
- What distracts you most when you are trying to focus on the present moment?
- What helps you return you attention once you have been distracted?

Chapter 7: Mindfulness of Thoughts

Tool 7-1: Flowing Stream

THEORY: A key aspect of mindfulness practice is being able to notice distractions and let go of them without engaging in them. This tool uses the imagination to notice a steady stream of objects (thoughts) while continuously letting them go by. It provides a great way to practice "letting go."

IMPLEMENTATION: Explain to the client that the goal of this tool is to practice letting go of thoughts without engaging with them. Read the Flowing Stream meditation in Handout 7-1.

PROCESSING: When the exercise is over, ask the client what they saw in their imagination. Did they have a hard time "letting go" of objects on the stream? Ask them what they did to keep from getting distracted. Did they see lots of types of things floating by or did the same thing come by over and over? What did they notice about how they felt while they watched the stream? Did the objects translate into thoughts?

HANDOUT 7-1
FLOWING STREAM

Get comfortable in your chair. Close your eyes and clear your mind. I want you to picture a stream with water lazily flowing by. As you look more closely at the water, you notice leaves, twigs, fish, and tiny objects of all different sizes, shapes, and colors flowing continuously by.

Now picture yourself standing beside the stream, watching everything coming toward you. Imagine that what you are watching for are your thoughts, wishes, feelings, or sensations. Watch them come downstream. As they come closer to you, just watch them come and go and get back to watching to see what comes down the stream next.

Try not to attach to or push away what you notice on the stream. Just let it come and let it go.

Continue for a few moments. (Note: Start with 30 seconds and work up to 5 minutes.)

When you are ready, open your eyes and bring your attention back to the room.

Tool 7-2: Mindfulness of Thoughts

THEORY: While practicing any mindfulness exercise, thoughts will emerge. With 60,000 thoughts a day, it is normal for thoughts to pop up while we are meditating. One of the key skills in mindfulness practice is noticing the thoughts, acknowledging them, and then dismissing them without engaging in them. This tool provides an effective method for dismissing thoughts.

IMPLEMENTATION: Explain that it is normal to have distracting thoughts while practicing mindfulness meditation. Describe the process for noticing thoughts and then dismissing them without engaging in them.

1. Observe the thought.
2. Accept the thought.
3. Let go of the thought—say, "Not now."

Don't get involved with the thought, just observe it.

Don't judge the thought or the fact that you had the thought. Accept and dismiss it.

Once you have taught this concept, read the Mindfulness of Thoughts meditation in Handout 7-2.

PROCESSING: Ask the client what this exercise was like for them. Did they have thoughts to write on the board? Were the thoughts in words or pictures? Was there any theme to the thoughts? Did they experience an inner dialogue commenting on the process of erasing the thought? Ask them what it feels like to know it's perfectly normal to have a steady flow of thoughts and that they can control whether they engage with them or not.

HANDOUT 7-2
MINDFULNESS OF THOUGHTS

Close your eyes and take a deep cleansing breath in through your nose and out through your mouth. Do it again. Inhale peace and comfort, exhale tension and stress. Allow the breath to come and go effortlessly. Be aware of the ease with which your breath comes and goes.

It is normal while you focus on your breath that thoughts will arise. They will come and go in a steady stream. For this mindfulness of thoughts meditation notice each thought as it arises.

Imagine you are looking at a blank white board right up in front of you. As you notice and acknowledge each thought, imagine that the thought is being written on the white board in bright red letters. As soon as it is written there, imagine that it simply vanishes off the board, poof. The board is white and blank again. When another thought arises, notice it, write it on the white board, and again, watch it vanish with a poof. Gone. You let it go. No need to engage with the thought or to judge it. Just notice it, watch it get written on the board, and watch it vanish.

Instead of thoughts being written on the board using words, you might imagine the thought being represented by a picture. As soon as the picture appears, imagine that it disappears instantly.

Do this over and over as the parade of thoughts continues. Enjoy the process of awareness of thoughts followed by their instantaneous disappearance. In between the thoughts bring your awareness back to your breath, your life force, your energy.

Continue this process on your own for the next 2 minutes.

Silence for 2 minutes. (Note: Vary this time to suit client's needs.)

Tool 7-3: Get in Between Thoughts

THEORY: Getting in Between Thoughts is a tool based on Wayne Dyer's "Getting in the Gap" meditation (Dyer, 2002). It is a practice based on visualizing two words and paying attention to the space between the words. It is a way to slow down the busy brain, focus on the gaps as opposed to the thoughts, clarify the thoughts, and get in touch with our inner being as well as God.

IMPLEMENTATION: Use Handout 7-3 to explain the process to your client. Choose or ask the client to write a positive affirmation that applies to their situation and then use their affirmation to do the meditation as outlined on the handout.

PROCESSING: Ask your client what they noticed when they did this meditation. What did they like about it? Were they able to visualize the words and focus on the gap between them? How did it feel to vocalize "AHH"? How did they feel about the affirmation? How did this meditation compare to the other ones they've done so far?

HANDOUT 7-3
GETTING IN BETWEEN THOUGHTS

Adapted from concept presented in *Getting in the Gap* by Wayne Dyer (Dyer, 2002).

The Getting in Between Thoughts meditation involves learning to focus on the gap between thoughts for a brief moment. It can be compared to the rest in music. It clarifies the thoughts. Wayne Dyer states that the gap is the source of creation.

The meditation utilizes the sound "AHH," which Wayne Dyer states is the basic sound for God around the world (God, Buddha, Mohammed, Allah, Krishna, Jehovah, Ra, etc.). Choose a positive relevant affirmation to use during the exercise. Wayne Dyer uses the first 10 words of the Lord's Prayer. Use that if it's appropriate for your specific client. If not, write an 8- to 10-word statement with your client that positively affirms the process that particular client is experiencing. Here are some examples:

- Lord's Prayer:
    - "Our Father, who art in heaven, hallowed be thy name."
- Learning to be mindful:
    - "My mindfulness skills are improving. I feel better and better."
    - "I am happy that I am getting better at mindfulness."
    - "Mindfulness improves my sense of well-being."
- Depression:
    - "I'm learning to find a thought that feels better."
    - "I'm glad I am learning how to feel better."
- Anxiety:
    - "I am learning to replace anxious thoughts with calm thoughts."
    - "I am grateful I am learning to regulate my worry."
- ADHD:
    - "Mindfulness helps me concentrate and stay calmer."
    - "Even though it's hard, being mindful is getting easier."
- Sleep Disorder:
    - "Mindfulness helps me fall and stay asleep every night."

The process is as follows. Substitute the words in the affirmation for your particular client.

Picture the first word in your mind's eye. Now that you can see it, move it to the left of your field of vision in your imagination. Now picture the second word in your mind's eye. Move it to the right of your field of vision. Now imagine that you are between the two words and focus on the space between the words. Take a deep breath and sing "AHH" as you slowly exhale. Take another deep breath and sing "AHH" as you exhale. Now picture the second word and move it over to the left to replace the first word. Now picture the third word and place it to the right.

Again, focus on the space between the two words. Take a deep breath and sing "AHH" on the exhale. Do it again. "AHH." Now move the third word to the left and place the fourth word on the right.

Again, focus on the space between the two words. Take a deep breath and sing "AHHH" on the exhale. Do it again. "AHH." Now move the fourth word to the left and place the fifth word on the right.

Repeat this process until all the words have been done.

Here's an example using a 4-word affirmation: "I enjoy being mindful."

Picture the word "I" in your mind's eye. Now that you can see it, move it to the left of your field of vision in your imagination. Now picture the word "enjoy" in your mind's eye. Move it to the right of your field of vision. Now imagine that you are between the two words with "I" on the left and "enjoy" on the right. Focus on the space between the words. Take a deep breath and sing "AHH" as you exhale. Take another deep breath and sing "AHH" as you exhale. Now picture the word "enjoy" and move it over to the left to replace the word "I." Now picture the word "being" and place it to the right.

Again, picture "enjoy" on the left and "being" on the right. Focus on the space between the two words. Take a deep breath and sing "AHH" on the exhale. Do it again. "AHH." Now move the word "being" to the left and place the word "mindful" on the right.

Again, focus on the space between the two words. Take a deep breath and sing "AHH" on the exhale. Do it again. "AHH."

Tool 7-4: Changing the Channel

THEORY: We can deliberately choose what we want to think about. This tool uses the concept that the current content of our thoughts is the channel we are watching. For example, we may be watching our worry, anger, sad, or stressed channel. We can change the channel to a more pleasant channel and thereby change the contents of our thoughts. This aligns with the cognitive behavioral concept that what we think about affects our feelings and our behavior and vice versa. And that we can choose a thought that feels better.

IMPLEMENTATION: Explain to clients the concept that their thoughts indicate what channel they are watching, such as happy, sad, worried, angry, calm, or stressed channel. Help your client identify the thoughts and the channel they are currently watching. Ask them to think about what they would put on their happy/peaceful/relaxed channel. Help them come up with positive ideas based on what you know about their interests and hobbies. Follow the process in Handout 7-4. Encourage them to use this tool whenever they need to shift their thoughts or feelings.

PROCESSING: Ask your client when they used this tool. How was it helpful? Were they able to identify negative/unpleasant thoughts in the moment? What did they put on their happy/peaceful/relaxed channel? What did they notice about their thoughts or mood when they used it? Do they need several different positive channels or is one enough?

Think about what you would put on your happy/peaceful/relaxed channel. Be specific.

Tune in to the content of your current thoughts.

Identify the thoughts as calm, happy, sad, worried, angry, etc. This is the channel you are currently watching.

If current thoughts feel bad or are negative, then imagine using the remote control to deliberately "change the channel" to your happy/peaceful/relaxed channel and imagine you are watching what you already decided would be on that channel.

Use this process any time you have negative or unpleasant thoughts or feelings.

CASE EXAMPLE:
A 7-year-old girl was extremely anxious at school and often panicky. Her anxiety was impacting her ability to stay in school, and she was being teased relentlessly by her peers.

She decided she would like to have "dancing" on her happy/peace/relaxed channel as she loved to dance.

Every time she noticed she was anxious, she imagined that she was changing the channel in her mind from her "worry channel" to her "happy/peace/relaxed channel."

Within a couple of weeks of starting this practice, her anxiety had almost disappeared. She was able to stay in school and her peers amazingly quit teasing her.

Tool 7-5: Automatic Negative Thoughts

THEORY: Many clients are experts at generating a steady stream of automatic negative thoughts. This is particularly true in depression, anxiety, and ADHD. Many of these negative thoughts originate from false core beliefs that get programmed into the brain very early, ostensibly for survival. Many people internalize the negative messages that they receive from their world. A 6-year-old boy told me his ADHD medicine was working because "no one yelled at me all day." Already, at 6, he felt bad about himself and experienced negative self-talk. Cognitive behavioral therapy works to identify and change these automatic negative thoughts. Daniel Amen calls these automatic negative thoughts "ANTs" and categorizes them into "species of ANTs" (Amen, 1998). This tool uses Amen's framework to identify automatic negative thoughts (ANTs) and to exterminate the ANTs by replacing them with realistic thoughts that feel better.

IMPLEMENTATION: In order to exterminate an automatic negative thought (ANT), we must first identify the ANT and then exterminate it by replacing it with a more positive reality-based thought. Review Handout 7-5A with your client and help them identify some of their automatic thoughts. Help them categorize their thought by ANT species. Then help them exterminate the ANT by replacing it with a positive thought that feels better using Handout 7-5B for examples. Encourage them to post the ANT graphic on Handout 7-5C someplace to remind them to be mindful of and exterminate their ANTs.

PROCESSING: Ask your client what ANTs they have become mindful of. Do they see a pattern of negative thinking? What species of ANTs have they identified? Explore how they have begun to replace the ANTs with thoughts that feel better. Where did they post the ANT graphic?

HANDOUT 7-5A
SPECIES OF AUTOMATIC NEGATIVE THOUGHTS (ANTs)

- **All-or-nothing thinking.** You see everything as entirely good or entirely bad: If you don't do something perfectly, you've failed.
- **Always/Never thinking.** You attribute a single negative event as part of a pattern. For example, you *always* forget to pay your bills.
- **Mind-reading.** You think you know what people think about you or something you've done without asking them—and it's usually bad.
- **Fortune-telling.** You are certain that things will turn out badly.
- **Magnification and minimization.** You exaggerate the significance of minor problems while trivializing your accomplishments.
- **Guilt-beating with "should" statements.** You focus on how things *should* be, leading to severe self-criticism as well as feelings of resentment toward others.
- **Personalizing.** You take everything personally.
- **Focusing on the negative.** You see only the negative aspects of any experience.
- **Emotional reasoning.** You assume that your negative feelings reflect reality. Feeling bad about your job means "I'm doing badly and will probably get fired."
- **Comparative thinking.** You measure yourself against others and feel inferior, even though the comparison may be unrealistic.
- **Labeling.** You attach a negative label to yourself or to someone else.
- **Blaming.** You blame someone else for your own problems. It's always someone else's fault.

HANDOUT 7-5B
EXTERMINATE THE ANT

SPECIES	EXAMPLE	KILL THE ANT
Always/Never Thinking	You are always late.	Sometimes you are late, but you always try to be on time.
Blaming	It's your fault we are late.	I could have met you to speed things up.
Personalizing	Taking something personally when it wasn't about you.	Maybe she didn't say hello because she is upset about her exam.
Labeling	I'm fat.	I would like to be thinner.
Guilt-beating	I shouldn't feel this way.	I understand why I feel this way.
Mind-reading	My teammates think I'm stupid.	Maybe they don't know me well yet.
Fortune-telling	We'll never find a parking space.	We'll find the closest one available.
Focusing on the negative	It's so cold outside.	The sun is beautiful.

Copy the ANT graphic and hang it up where you will see it to remind yourself to be mindful of your own ANTs.

Tool 7-6: Journal About Being Mindful of Thoughts

THEORY: One key aspect of mindfulness practice is to notice thoughts and to let them go without engaging. Another component of mindfulness is increasing awareness of the content of the thoughts and the ability to change negative thoughts to thoughts that feel better. This tool will help the client explore this process.

IMPLEMENTATION: Explain to the client that mindfulness practice starts with noticing thoughts and dismissing them without engaging, which eventually increases the ability to monitor the thought content and gradually change the automatic negative thoughts (ANTs) to thoughts that feel better. Ask the client to respond to the journal prompts in Handout 7-6.

PROCESSING: Explore the client's answers with them. If they didn't write anything, go over the questions with them in session and discuss their responses. Help the client identify how mindfulness practice is helping them.

HANDOUT 7-6
JOURNAL ABOUT BEING MINDFUL OF THOUGHTS

Journal Prompts:

- What's it like for you to notice thoughts and not engage with them?
- Do you notice any change in mood when you dismiss thoughts during mindfulness practice?
- Have you experienced any calming during mindfulness practice?
- Do certain thoughts tend to recur?
- Have you noticed any change in your ability to let go of thoughts while practicing mindfulness?
- Do you see a pattern of automatic negative thinking?
- What's your sense of where this pattern started in your life?
- What species of ANTs have you identified?
- Describe an example of when you had success with finding thoughts that feel better.
- How have the Mindfulness of Thoughts meditations helped you?

Chapter 8: Mindfulness of Emotions

Tool 8-1: Awareness of Emotions

THEORY: There are three basic components to an emotion to be mindful of:

- Thoughts (or the story behind the emotion)
- Physical sensations: how the emotion manifests itself in the body. All emotions have some physical component. This is often how we know that we are having an emotion.
- Emotional mood or tone in the mind. This can be subtle, or quite obvious.

We can pay attention to any of these aspects of the emotion in mindfulness.

The thoughts or the story that accompanies the emotion often tends to pull us in so that we lose our mindfulness. These thoughts or story usually pertain to the past or future—not the present, and hence divert us from being mindful of the present.

This tool provides a simple process for being mindful of emotions, identifying the emotion without judging, and examining the present moment of the feeling without getting pulled into the past or future.

IMPLEMENTATION: Explain the process of mindfulness of emotions process as outlined in Handout 8-1. Help your client identify feelings, observe them without judging or trying to change them, notice where the emotion manifests in their body, and clarify what is present versus past or future. If the client states that they aren't feeling anything in particular in the moment, then ask them to explore the process by remembering an emotion they experienced recently.

PROCESSING: Ask your client what it was like to focus on their emotions as an observer. Where they able to identify and name the emotion? Where did the emotion show up in their body? Where they able to identify the present component of the emotion as well as the past or future components? What thoughts triggered their emotion? What was their story behind the feeling?

HANDOUT 8-1
AWARENESS OF EMOTIONS PROCESS

- Notice the feeling.
    - Identify the feeling—name it.
    - Notice how and where it shows up in your body.

- Observe the feeling as:
    - Pleasant, unpleasant, neutral

- Accept the feeling—don't judge it or try to change it.

- Investigate the present moment of the feeling.
    - Notice the component of the emotion that is present as well as those aspects that are past or future aspects of the feeling.

- Stay present with it.

- Don't identify with the feeling.
    - Your emotion does not equal you.

- Examine the thoughts and the story behind the feeling.

- Identify the trigger for this emotion.

- When have you experienced this emotion before?

Tool 8-2: Meditation: Mindfulness of Emotions

THEORY: Basic mindfulness practice involves letting go of thoughts and emotions that arise during practice. This more advanced tool goes a step further to help the client tune into an emotion as it arises, observe it, examine it, and notice how and where it shows up in their body. By cultivating such mindfulness of emotions, we can build our resiliency to handle the intense experiences associated with daily life. We can decrease our tendency to get hijacked by emotions, which can sidetrack us and lead us to undesired places (like taking the wrong highway exit).

IMPLEMENTATION: Explain that the purpose of this exercise is to increase the client's ability to tune into an emotion, observe it without judging, and notice where and how it shows up in their body. Ask the client to find a comfortable position and close their eyes if they feel comfortable doing so. Read the Mindfulness of Emotions Meditation in Handout 8-2. Then help them reflect on what came up for them.

PROCESSING: Reflection on what came up during a meditation is important, as it helps the client get the most benefit from the practice. Ask them what this exercise was like for them. Did they notice an emotion that arose during the practice? Where they able to identify it? What was it? Where did they notice it in their body? Give them some examples such as stomach ache, muscle tension, changes in heart rate or body temperature. Were they distracted and, if so, how did they bring their attention back to their emotion? What triggered the emotion? When have they experienced it before? What was the story behind the emotion? Was it past, present, or future?

HANDOUT 8-2
MINDFULNESS OF EMOTIONS MEDITATION

We all experience emotions continuously throughout the day. They often start as a small nudge, gradually increase in intensity and then decrease. This is much like the waves in the surf at the ocean shore. They start slowly offshore, build as they come into shore, and then slowly recede only to be replaced by new waves in a continuous cycle.

This exercise will help you tune into your emotions, your judgments about them, and their wavelike ebb and flow.

- Take a few moments to focus on your breathing.
- Just notice your breathing without changing it.
- Pause.
- Notice how you feel emotionally in the present moment.
- Without judging just be aware of how you feel.
- What feeling are you experiencing?
- Name the feeling.
- It is pleasant or unpleasant?
- Notice if it feels good or not good.
- Is the feeling steady or coming and going?
- It is changing in intensity?
- How is it changing?
- Gently maintain your attention on your emotion.
- Have you felt this emotion before?
- Is it coming from the past or the present?
- What is the present moment of the emotion.
- How are you breathing?
- How does your posture match the feeling?
- How does the emotion show up in your body?
- Is there any part of your body that is uncomfortable?
- Have you noticed this body sensation before?
- Are your muscles tense or relaxed?
- What is your facial expression?
- As you notice thoughts simply acknowledge them, dismiss them and bring your attention back to your emotion.
- Allow and accept instead of judging.
- As one emotion subsides and another emotion arises simply repeat the process.
- Allow, accept, and name the feeling.
- Remind yourself that you are not your emotion.
- Investigate the present moment of the emotion.

- Do you tend to hold onto certain emotions?
- Do you reject others?
- How can you replace a negative emotion with a positive one?
- Bring your attention to your breath.
- Reflect on what came up for you during this meditation.

Inspired by Jonathan Kaplan, PhD (Kaplan, 2008)

Tool 8-3: Core Heart Feelings

THEORY: Studies have shown that depression and anxiety improve when people practice putting their heart into coherence by imagining core heart feelings. In fact, core heart feelings actually play a greater role in increasing our health and longevity than age, blood pressure, cholesterol, or smoking (Childre et al., 1999). One commercially available computer program, HeartMath's EmWave™ program (HearthMath, 2013), allows you to see your heart rate variability improve as you imagine feelings of appreciation, gratitude, love, or caring. This tool provides the technique that has been proven to put the heart into coherence.

IMPLEMENTATION: Explain how we can change heart rate variability in very positive ways by simply focusing on the heart area and remembering a feeling of appreciation, gratitude, love, or caring. Read Handout 8-3 to your client and reflect on what came up for them. Ask them to practice this during the week.

PROCESSING: Help your client reflect on what this mindfulness practice was like for them. What feeling of appreciation, gratitude, love, or caring did they remember? What did it feel like to focus on their heart area? What changes in their breathing, or physical sensations, did they notice? How did they feel different after doing the exercise?

HANDOUT 8-3
CORE HEART FEELINGS

Here is a simple exercise to put your heart into coherence.

Find a comfortable position where you won't be disturbed for a few minutes.

Close your eyes and take a few deep breaths in through your nose to the count of four and exhale slowly through pursed lips to the count of eight.

Clear your mind and bring your attention to your heart area.

Pretend you are breathing slowly through your heart.

Now remember a time when you felt appreciation and gratitude for someone or something positive in your life—perhaps remember the feeling of love or caring for someone.

Send that feeling of appreciation to yourself and others.

Feel the feeling and stay with it.

As other thoughts pop into your mind, just dismiss each thought and gently bring your attention back to the area around your heart.

Continue doing this for 5-10 minutes.

(Adapted from HeartMath workshop) (Childre et al., 1999)

Tool 8-4: Journal About Mindfulness of Emotions

THEORY: Mindfulness of emotions practice improves the ability to notice emotions as they arise. It increases emotional self-regulation and resiliency. Now that your client has practiced these skills, journaling will help them consolidate their learning.

IMPLEMENTATION: Explain to your client why journaling is an important way to increase the effectiveness of their practice. Ask them to respond to the journal prompts in Handout 8-4, either in writing (or with drawing) or verbally.

PROCESSING: Review your client's answers to the journal prompts with them. Ask them what they have learned from practicing the mindfulness skills and journaling about their experience.

HANDOUT 8-4
JOURNAL ABOUT MINDFULNESS OF EMOTIONS

Journal Prompts:

- What emotions did you notice arising during this practice?
- Were you able to notice where the emotion showed up in your body?
- Were you able to observe without judging or engaging in the emotion?
- Did you identify the trigger for the emotion?
- What was the story behind it?
- What was it like to sort out the present moment of the emotion from the past or future component?
- What did you do to stay present?
- How did you handle distracting thoughts?
- What feeling of appreciation or gratitude did you remember?
- What did you notice about your emotional state when you deliberately focused on your heart and remembered a feeling of appreciation?
- How did your physical state change during the core heart feelings meditation?
- How did you feel after practicing the core heart feelings meditation?
- How is your mindfulness practice helping you?

Chapter 9: Mindfulness of Physical Body

Tool 9-1: Body Scan

THEORY: The Body Scan Meditation is routinely included in studies on the effectiveness of mindfulness. It is a component of most formal meditation practices such as Jon Kabat-Zinn's Mindfulness Based Stress Reduction Program (Kabat-Zinn, 2012). It involves focusing your full attention on each part of the body, noticing whatever sensations arise, accepting them, and sending kind and compassionate thoughts to each area of the body. Through regular practice, it can help you to enter deep states of relaxation, accept your body as it is, work effectively with body sensations and feelings of discomfort and pain, and increase powers of concentration and mindfulness.

IMPLEMENTATION: Explain to clients that a body scan is a common component of many formal mindfulness mediation practices. It is designed to help them enter a deep state of relaxation, to accept their body as it is, work with discomfort and pain, and increase concentration and mindfulness. Read through Handout 9-1 with your client lying on their back if at all possible, or sitting comfortably in a chair. Encourage them to practice this between sessions. If they become uncomfortable or emotional at any point, ask them if they want to continue or to stop.

PROCESSING: Help your client reflect on how they felt during and after practicing the Body Scan Meditation. What did they notice about their body? Were they able to stay focused? Did they fall asleep? Did they become more relaxed or more agitated? What was it like for them to simply observe and accept? Did any thoughts or emotions arise when they focused on specific areas of their body? If so, process these and help them connect them to past experiences. It is not uncommon for people who have experienced trauma to remember deeply buried feelings or thoughts when they focus on certain parts of their body. If they need to stop, process what came up for them. Help them to integrate the past memory with the safety of this moment.

HANDOUT 9-1
BODY SCAN

Let's begin. Breathe in slowly through your nose to the count of four: 1-2-3-4 and breathe out through your mouth even more slowly like you are blowing a huge bubble, to the count of eight: 1-2-3-4-5-6-7-8. Now just breathe normally.

Bring your attention to you left foot. Just notice your left foot including your toes, heel, bottom of your left foot, top of your left foot. Notice what it feels like. Then move up to your left ankle. Notice how your left ankle feels. Pay attention to whether there is any pain there, is it cold, or hot, does it feel light or heavy? Accept the sensations as you become aware of them.

Then pay attention to your left leg, starting at the bottom, up to your knees, and thighs, all the way to your hips at the top of your leg. Notice if your left leg feels tight or relaxed, warm or cold, light or heavy. Send loving, compassionate thoughts to your left leg starting from your foot right on up to the top of your thighs.

Now pay attention to your right foot. Just notice your right foot, including your toes, heel, bottom of your right foot, top of your right foot. Notice what it feels like. Then move up to your right ankle. Notice how your right ankle feels. Pay attention to whether there is any pain there, is it cold, or hot, does it feel light or heavy? Then pay attention to your right leg starting at the bottom, up to your knees, and thighs, all the way to your hips at the top of your leg. Notice if it feels tight or relaxed, warm or cold, light or heavy. Send warm thoughts of gratitude to your entire right leg.

Now pay attention to both legs from your toes up to your hips. Be still, breathe, and send your legs some kind and loving thoughts. Breathe gently into your legs.

Now move your attention to your belly. Just observe what's there. Notice how your belly feels. Let it be the way it is. Send love and kindness to your belly.

Now pay attention to your back, starting with your low back all the way up to your shoulders. Notice any sensations present in your back. Send warm thoughts of relaxation to your back. Sit for a moment just noticing everything about your back.

Now give your attention to your fingers, thumbs, wrists. Observe what your hands are carrying. Send thoughts of gratitude and compassion to your hard-working hands. Now focus on your arms from your wrists all the way up to your shoulders. Just notice what's there.

Remember to breathe.

Now pay attention to your neck and throat. Swallow and notice how your neck and throat feel. As you observe your neck and throat, send thoughts of health and healing to this area of your body.

Now pay attention to your face: your chin, your mouth, your cheeks, your eyes, your eyebrows, your forehead, and finally your ears. Take a moment to observe what's there. Notice everything without attempting to change it. Send thoughts of love and kindness to your face. Allow a smile to emerge.

Now bring your attention to your head, including your hair and scalp and your brain inside your head. Observe the activity inside your mind. Send thoughts of kindness and connection. Connect with your inner wisdom.

Now take a deep belly breath and fill your whole body with a cushion of healing energy. As you blow the air out gently, let go of anything that needs to go.

Slowly open your eyes and bring your attention back to the room.

Tool 9-2: Relaxation Response

THEORY: The term "relaxation response" was coined by Herbert Benson, M.D., at Harvard Medical School (Benson, 2000). This meditation invokes the relaxation response, which effectively decreases the stress response. Although many of the mindfulness tools may foster the relaxation response, the meditation included here was designed specifically for this purpose.

IMPLEMENTATION: Explain to your client that this meditation invokes the relaxation response, which is a term coined by Herbert Benson, M.D., at Harvard Medical School. The relaxation response is a perfect antidote to the negative effects of the stress response. Ask your client to find a comfortable position and then lead them using the meditation from Handout 9-2. Depending on your client's experience with meditation, vary the length of the pause between 30 seconds and several minutes.

PROCESSING: Help your client reflect on what they experienced during this meditation. Did they notice a feeling of relaxation? What did it feel like? Is this a new or a familiar feeling? Did they feel drowsy or fall asleep? Did they notice any particular sensations in their body? Did their body seem to become numb, float, or disappear from awareness? Were they able to maintain their focus for the whole time? Could they do it for a longer period of time, or was this already too long?

HANDOUT 9-2
RELAXATION RESPONSE

The Relaxation Response is a simple practice that, once learned, can help relieve stress and tension. Learning and putting into practice such techniques can significantly improve your mental, emotional, and physical health.

The term Relaxation Response was coined by Herbert Benson, M.D., at Harvard Medical School (Benson, 2000). Read the following meditation to clients to effectively invoke the Relaxation Response. Depending on the client's experience with meditation, vary the pause near the end between 30 seconds and several minutes.

Find yourself a comfortable position either sitting in a chair with feet flat on the floor, hands on thighs with palms facing up; or lying on your back with arms and legs uncrossed and arms lying by your side palms up.

Now take a deep breath in through your nose to the count of 4 and exhale through your mouth like you are blowing a bubble to the count of 8. Do it again. Breathe in relaxation and peace. As you exhale relax your mind and exhale tension and worry. Do it one more time, inhale a cushion of healing energy and as you exhale relax your body.

Now bring your attention to your feet. Notice what you carry there in your toes, arches, heels, and balls and tops of your feet. Let go of anything that needs to go and let it flow down through the ends of your toes and onto the floor.

Now focus on your ankles. Notice if there is any tightness or discomfort and let it flow down through your feet, right through the ends of your toes and onto the floor.

Now bring your attention to you calves and shins. Just notice what's there and let go of anything that needs to go. Let it flow down through your ankles, through your feet, and right out through the ends of your toes and onto the floor.

Now pay attention to your knees. Notice what's there and let healing energy flow down from your knees through your calves and shins, through your feet, and right through the ends of your toes and onto the floor.

Now bring your awareness to your thighs, fronts, backs, sides, and insides. Release anything that needs to go and let it flow down through your knees, through your calves and shins, through your feet, and right through the ends of your toes and onto the floor.

Concentrate on your bottom. Move back and forth ever so slightly to release tension stored there. Let it flow down through your thighs, through your knees, through your calves and shins, through your feet, and right through the ends of your toes and onto the floor.

Now focus on your entire legs and feet. Take a slow, deep breath and fill your legs and feet with a cushion of healing energy. As you exhale slowly let anything that needs to go flow gently out with your breath.

Now pay attention to your lower back. Lots of stuff gets carried here and you just don't need any of it. Let it flow down through your bottom, through your thighs, through your knees, through your calves and shins, through your feet, and right through the ends of your toes and onto the floor.

Pay attention to your abdomen and notice how it feels. Let go of any tightness or discomfort and let it flow down through your thighs, through your knees, through your calves and shins, through your feet, and right through the ends of your toes and onto the floor.

Now bring your awareness to your stomach area. Picture in your mind's eye a rope that is twisted, coiled and tied in a tight knot. As you watch this rope it un-ties, uncoils, untwists until it is hanging limply. Imagine this happening to your stomach area as your release tension there and let it flow down through your abdomen, through your thighs, through your knees, through your calves and shins, through your feet, and right through the ends of your toes and onto the floor.

Now focus on your chest. Take a deep breath and fill your lungs with a cushion of healing air and as you exhale release anything that needs to go. Do it again, inhale peace and comfort and as you exhale relax your mind and body.

Bring your focus to your heart. Inhale through your heart and imagine feelings of appreciation and gratitude. Spend a moment here.

Now bring your attention to your back, your middle and upper back. Lots of tension gets stored here and you don't need it. Let it flow down through your lower back, your bottom, your thighs, your knees, your calves and shins, your feet, and right through the ends of your toes and onto the floor.

Now focus on your shoulders, throat and neck. Move your head back and forth ever so gently to release the tension stored there. Let it flow down through your back, your lower back, your bottom, your thighs, your knees, your calves and shins, your feet, and right through the ends of your toes and onto the floor.

Now pay attention to your hands including your fingers, thumbs, palms, and the backs of your hands. Notice what you are carrying there and let go of anything that needs to be let go. Let it flow right through the ends of your fingers and onto the floor.

Pay attention to your arms from your shoulders, upper arms, elbows, forearms, and wrists. Let any tightness stored there flow down through your arms and wrists, hands and right through the ends of your fingers and onto the floor.

Bring your attention to your face and jaw. Tighten up your checks into a huge smile and hold for a few seconds then let go. Now scrunch up your forehead and close your eyes tight, tight, tight, and then release. Relax your jaw, open your mouth slightly and allow your jaw to hang loosely. Place your tongue lightly on the bottom of your mouth behind your lower teeth. Feel the release in your jaw. Expand your awareness to your scalp from your forehead down to your ears and around to the base of your skull. Let any tension that was stored in your face, jaw and scalp flow down through your chest, abdomen, legs, feet, and right through the ends of your toes and onto the floor.

Now take a quick inventory of your body and notice any areas of discomfort or tightness. Take a deep breath in through your nose and fill those areas of your body with a cushion of healing energy and let it flow out as your exhale slowly through your mouth. Do it again. Inhale a cushion of light and healing and then exhale anything that needs to go.

Now that your whole body is relaxed, know that every part of your body is working exactly as it was designed to work. Blood and energy are flowing freely bringing healing, oxygen and nutrients to every part of your body. Tune in to this feeling of total relaxation.

Enjoy this warm, safe place for a few minutes.

Pause. (Vary this time to suit client needs)

When you are ready slowly bring your awareness back to the room. Open your eyes when you are ready.

Bring this relaxed feeling with you as you return to alertness. Remember this feeling any time you need to invoke your relaxation response.

Tool 9-3: Progressive Muscle Relaxation

THEORY: Progressive muscle relaxation is a systematic technique for achieving a deep state of relaxation. It was developed by Dr. Edmund Jacobson more than 50 years ago (Jacobson, 2012). Dr. Jacobson discovered that a muscle could be relaxed by first tensing it for a few seconds and then releasing it. Tensing and releasing various muscle groups throughout the body produces a deep state of relaxation, which Dr. Jacobson found capable of relieving a variety of conditions, from high blood pressure to ulcerative colitis.

Keep in mind that the body can be relaxed at the same time the brain is alert. This is the definition of peak performance. Practicing progressive relaxation leads to the ability to evoke a physical relaxation on demand in a few moments just by remembering how the body felt at the end of the relaxation meditation and doing two or three deep cleansing breaths to invoke it.

IMPLEMENTATION: Read the following explanation to your client. Progressive muscle relaxation is a systematic technique for achieving a deep state of relaxation. Dr. Jacobsen's progressive muscle relaxation involves tensing and relaxing, in succession, 16 different muscle groups of the body. The idea is to tense each muscle group hard (without straining) for about 10 seconds, and then to let go of it suddenly. Then relax for 15 to 20 seconds, noticing how the muscle group feels when relaxed in contrast to how it felt when tensed, before going on to the next group of muscles. You might also say to yourself: "Relaxing, relaxing," "Letting go, letting go," "Letting go of everything that needs to go," or any other relaxing phrase during each relaxation period between successive muscle groups. Throughout the exercise, maintain your focus on your muscles. When your attention wanders, bring it back to the particular muscle group you're working on.

Read Handout 9-3 to your client and demonstrate each muscle group for them as you go along. Reflect on their experience afterward. Encourage them to practice this at home on their own.

PROCESSING: Ask your client to reflect on what they experienced while doing the Progressive Muscle Relaxation Meditation. Were they able to notice the difference between a tense muscle and a relaxed muscle? Did they feel more relaxed at the end of the meditation? How did they handle distracting thoughts? Did they experience any particular emotions during the exercise? In what ways does practicing this mindfulness technique help them?

HANDOUT 9-3
PROGRESSIVE MUSCLE RELAXATION

Find yourself a comfortable position.

1. To begin, take three deep belly breaths, exhaling slowly each time. As you exhale, imagine that tension throughout your body begins to flow away.
2. Clench your fists. Hold for 7–10 seconds and then release for 15–20 seconds. Use these same time intervals for all other muscle groups.
3. Tighten your biceps by drawing your forearms up toward your shoulders and "making a muscle" with both arms. Hold . . . and then relax.
4. Tighten your triceps—the muscles on the undersides of your upper arms—by extending your arms out straight and locking your elbows. Hold . . . and then relax.
5. Tighten the muscles in your forehead by raising your eyebrows as far as you can. Hold . . . and then relax. Imagine your forehead muscles becoming smooth and limp as they relax.
6. Tighten the muscles around your eyes by clenching your eyelids tightly shut. Hold . . . and then relax. Imagine sensations of deep relaxation spreading all around them.
7. Tighten your jaws by opening your mouth so widely that you stretch the muscles around the hinges of your jaw. Hold . . . and then relax. Let your lips part and allow your jaw to hang loose.
8. Tighten the muscles in the back of your neck by pulling your head way back, as if you were going to touch your head to your back (be gentle with this muscle group to avoid injury). Focus only on tensing the muscles in your neck. Hold . . . and then relax. Since this area is often especially tight, it's good to do the tighten–relax cycle twice.
9. Take a few deep breaths and tune in to the weight of your head sinking into whatever surface it is resting on.
10. Tighten your shoulders by raising them up as if you were going to touch your ears. Hold . . . and then relax.
11. Tighten the muscles around your shoulder blades by pushing your shoulder blades back as if you were going to touch them together. Hold the tension in your shoulder blades . . . and then relax. Since this area is often especially tight, you might repeat the tighten–relax sequence twice.
12. Tighten the muscles of your chest by taking in a deep breath. Hold for up to 10 seconds . . . and then release slowly. Imagine any excess tension in your chest flowing away with the exhalation.
13. Tighten your stomach muscles by sucking your stomach in. Hold . . . and then release. Imagine a wave of relaxation spreading through your abdomen.
14. Tighten your lower back by arching it up. Hold . . . and then relax.
15. Tighten your buttocks by pulling them together. Hold . . . and then relax. Imagine the muscles in your hips going loose and limp.
16. Squeeze the muscles in your thighs all the way down to your knees. You will probably have to tighten your hips along with your thighs, since the thigh muscles attach at the pelvis. Hold . . . and then relax. Feel your thigh muscles smoothing out and relaxing completely.
17. Tighten your calf muscles by pulling your toes toward you (flex carefully to avoid cramps). Hold . . . and then relax.
18. Tighten your feet by curling your toes downward. Hold . . . and then relax.
19. Now imagine a wave of relaxation slowly spreading throughout your body, starting at your head and gradually penetrating every muscle group all the way down to your toes.

This exercise was adapted from (Jacobson, 2012).

Tool 9-4: Remembered Wellness

THEORY: Herbert Benson, M.D., coined the term "remembered wellness" (Benson, 1996). "Remembered wellness" is what happens when you allow the body and mind to recover its memory of wholeness and completeness, of innate order, balance, harmony, and flow. Remembered wellness involves remembering a time when we felt well and reimagining what it felt like. Studies have shown that the body reacts to imagination and visualization as it does to an actual event, so it doesn't know the difference between an imagined wellness and a real wellness. This Remembered Wellness Tool helps the client tap into the power of their imagination through remembering a time when they felt well in order to create wellness in the present.

IMPLEMENTATION: Explain the concept of remembered wellness to your client. Discuss the power of using the imagination to recreate previous wellness in the present. Read the Remembered Wellness Meditation in Handout 9-4 to your client. Help your client reflect on the results. Encourage them to use this skill whenever they want to improve their current physical or emotional health, and repeatedly if dealing with chronic illness.

PROCESSING: Ask your client to reflect on how they experienced this meditation. Were they able to remember a time they felt well? How did they feel different than they do now? What did they notice in their feeling of wellness when they completed the meditation? Some clients become quite emotional during this meditation as they remember how good they used to feel and they get in touch with losses they have incurred due to decreases in physical or emotional health. Therefore, be prepared to process these feelings with them.

HANDOUT 9-4
REMEMBERED WELLNESS MEDITATION

Take a deep relaxing breath and focus your attention within.

Go inside.

Let your unconscious mind choose a time in your life, no matter how brief it was, when you felt really good.

Even if you had unpleasant things going on at the same time, just retrieve the memory of when you felt really well.

Be selective.

Choose only the best.

Remember that time.

Remember how you felt then.

Your muscles are in peak condition.

Your body is in excellent health.

Everything is working exactly as it was designed to work.

Your thoughts are positive and happy.

You experience a profound sense of well-being.

Your mood is content, calm, blissful, peaceful.

Use whatever the words are that best describe that state for you.

Breathe that memory in now.

Let it grow and intensify.

Remember it.

Feel it.

Allow it.

Build an inner wave of joy.

Smile.

Enjoy the memory as it spreads throughout your mind and body.

Notice how for the moment your brain doesn't know the difference between then and now.

Every cell, every muscle, every neuron, every fiber of your brain and body is remembering.

As you remember wellness, notice that it starts to spread.

Your body knows how to heal.

We've all fallen down and scraped ourselves, or cut ourselves,

And then healed.

Our bodies know absolutely how to heal.

You're remembering that peak state,

Physically, emotionally, spiritually, intellectually, and vibrationally.

Imagine bringing that feeling from when the memory occurred to right now.

Almost like a copy and paste from then to now.

Let your body feel, right now, that peak wellness.

Your memory is guiding your brain to function now like it did when you were well.

You might like to imagine a color that represents this incredible wellness.

What color would you choose?

The color anchors the feeling.

Imagine that color now.

Notice that there's a certain way you breathe that is all part of that healing process.

Begin to notice everyday all the ways your body shows you it knows how to heal.

Eating, breathing, sleeping, laughing, peeing, sweating.

Ask for a word or phrase that represents your peak wellness.

Allow every adjustment that is part of this peak health.

Find a place to be grateful for the way things are.

Be thankful that your body remembers wellness.

When you are ready, let yourself come gradually back to the room, and slowly all the way out.

Bring your remembered wellness with you.

Know that the remembered wellness starts a process that continues throughout the day, night, weeks, months, and on into your future.

As you return to the present, know that your remembered wellness has been activated and is now operating in the present.

Tool 9-5: Journal About Increasing Awareness of Physical Body

THEORY: These Mindfulness of Physical Body tools produce physical and emotional relaxation. They provide an excellent way to counter the stressors encountered in daily life. This journaling tool will help the client review what they have noticed while doing these meditations and increase their awareness of the positive benefits.

IMPLEMENTATION: Ask the client to respond to the journal prompts in Handout 9-5 either in writing or verbally.

PROCESSING: Review the client's journal responses with them. Process any emotional response they may have experienced during the meditation. Help them explore their new-found ability to relax as a tool they can use to deal with stress.

Journal Prompts:

- What has changed for you about the way you notice your body?
- Has your ability to observe and accept discomfort or pain changed?
- Do you feel more in control of body tension?
- What does it feel like to completely relax?
- Is relaxation a new feeling or a familiar one?
- Are you better able to relax your muscles at will?
- Did any particular emotions arise when you paid attention to your body?
- Did you experience a kind of cell memory of previous intense emotions or trauma?
- How did you handle these emotions as they arose?
- Where you able to feel safe being mindful of your body?
- Are you able to remember the feeling of the relaxation response when you start to feel stressed?

Chapter 10: Mindfulness of Relationships

Tool 10-1: Relationships

THEORY: Being mindful in relationships is essential to building healthy connections throughout the life span. Unfortunately, many people are so busy and distracted by competing demands that they do not give their complete and undivided attention to others they are talking with. This tool is designed to help people stop and think about a specific relationship and to help them improve their ability to be mindful in that relationship.

IMPLEMENTATION: All types of relationships can benefit from mindfulness. These include relationships with family, loved ones, significant others, friends, co-workers, bosses, employees, teachers, and even pets. Use Handout 10-1 as a guide to help clients examine a relationship of their choice (past, present, or future) and to give them the skills to stay present and use positive relationship skills while they are communicating with others. Tell them to substitute the person they are in relationship with (or an imagined future relationship) for "loved one" in the steps outlined in the exercise. Some clients will imagine a loved one they have lost. It is okay to leave this choice up to the client, but you may adapt this for the needs of your particular client.

PROCESSING: Assist clients in processing what came up for them during this exercise. Did they choose a person from the past, future, or present? What did they notice about their emotions while they practiced this process and answered the questions? Some clients will experience sadness as this exercise triggers feelings of loss for a deceased loved one or the absence of a love partner or regret about how they handled a relationship. Help them reflect on these emotions. What triggered the emotion? Explore what they learned from doing this mindfulness skill. Were any of the steps difficult for the client?

MINFULNESS OF RELATIONSHIPS

ELEVEN WAYS TO BE MINDFUL IN YOUR RELATIONSHIPS

All types of relationships can benefit from mindfulness. These include relationships with family, loved ones, significant others, friends, co-workers, bosses, employees, teachers, and so on. Substitute the person you are in a relationship with (or an imagined future relationship) for "loved one" in the following steps.

1. Stop what you are doing and be totally present with your loved one either in person or in your imagination. Listen to them. Look them in the eye. Smile at them. Give them your undivided attention. Let them know you think they are terrific. Avoid judgment. Show them your unconditional love and acceptance. Think of all the things you love about them.

2. Notice what thoughts or feelings arise in you as you think about your loved one. Acknowledge and accept the thoughts or feelings and then let them go.

3. Ask, "What does my loved one need from me right now?" Ask yourself how you can give them your unconditional love and acceptance. Tune in to their needs, as well as your own.

4. Try to see the world from your loved one's point of view. What stressors do they have? How would you feel if you were your loved one?

5. Write down your expectations for your relationship. Are your expectations realistic? Are they in your loved one's best interest? In yours?

6. Learn to accept your loved one exactly the way they are. Love them unconditionally. Let them know you love them no matter what. Look past their difficult behavior to the beautiful being underneath. They are already good enough.

7. Understand what your loved one is feeling. Validate their feelings.

8. Avoid the trap of constantly telling your loved one what to do or how to do it. Practice being in charge of yourself but not of your loved one.

9. When you need to represent yourself with your loved one, do it with love. Use "I" statements to say, "I think, I feel, I want." "I like it when . . . " Be positive, clear, and kind.

10. Practice compassion and some type of loving kindness mindfulness regularly. Allow yourself to be still. Be silent. Think about all the things you love, like, and are grateful for about your loved one. Focus on the positive.

11. Take care of yourself so you can be in the best condition to be mindful.

Tool 10-2: Mindful Listening for Feeling "Felt"

THEORY: In his book *Mindsight,* Dan Siegel discusses the concept of feeling "felt" by another person (Siegel, 2010). Siegel states that feeling "felt" is what happens when we allow our internal state to shift and come to resonate with the inner world of another. This is critical in attachment theory as the child needs to "feel felt" by their parent in order to attach, feel secure, and develop appropriately. It is also needed throughout life to feel known by and connected to others. This may be involved in activating mirror neurons, neurons that fire both when a person (or animal) acts and when the person observes the same action performed by another. Thus, the neuron "mirrors" the behavior of the other, as though the observer were itself acting.

This mindfulness tool is designed to teach the concept of "feeling felt" and give the client practice doing it. The practice of this skill will invariably improve relationships and connectedness. It is an excellent skill for all helping professionals and teachers to practice themselves to increase their attunement with their clients or students and thereby improve treatment outcomes.

IMPLEMENTATION: Review and practice this skill yourself and apply it whenever you interact with others. Then explain the definition of feeling "felt" to your client. Discuss the components of "feeling felt" listed in Handout 10-2. Then practice it with your client to help them "feel felt" right in your office. Then reverse roles and see if they can make you "feel felt."

PROCESSING: Help your client integrate this skill by doing it in session and then processing what it felt like to feel "felt." Help them understand it by experiencing it from your doing it for them in session. Then reverse roles and process what it felt like to make you "feel felt." Share how you felt when they did this.

HANDOUT 10-2
FEELING "FELT"

Feeling "Felt" is:
Feeling like someone else really knows you and understands you and has your best interest at heart. Feeling like they "get you."

How to help others feel "felt" by you:

- Be curious, interested, and open to the person.
- Let them know you care and want to know them.
- Spend time with them.
- Give them your full undivided attention. Make eye contact. Ignore distractions such as phone calls, text messages, and the like when you are with them.
- Practice being mindful of being present with them.
- Truly listen to them in an accepting and non-judgmental way.
- Repeat back what you just heard the person say to help them feel heard, understood, known, and "felt."
- Remember what they told you about themselves and mention it to them at another time.
- Take time to know how the person feels by listening when they tell you and by talking with them about their feelings.
- Be willing to be vulnerable and share your feelings, dreams, likes, dislikes.
- Tune in to how your mirror neurons resonate with them. For example, notice how you feel when you are with them. What changes do you notice in your emotional landscape, bodily sensations, or energy?
- Show them by your actions that you are on their side, their team.
- Help them out when they need help with something.
- Be mindful when you are with them and notice what they like to eat, what their favorite color is, what their habits are.
- Be trustworthy so they feel safe with you.
- Guard their secrets, and don't share them with others unless they tell you to.

Tool 10-3: Journal About the Last Time I Felt "Felt"

THEORY: The concept of feeling "felt" was introduced in Tool 10-2. This tool will help the client integrate what they learned as they explore what it was like for them to feel "felt."

IMPLEMENTATION: Review the concept of feeling "felt" with your client—Tool 10-2. Discuss how this concept impacts relationships, feeling connected, and feeling known. Ask your client to review and respond to the journal prompts in Handout 10-3.

PROCESSING: Review journal prompts with clients. Explore when they felt "felt." Discuss how they make others feel "felt." Ask them what they discovered about how they interact with others. Are they able to identify changes in their behavior that would help others feel "felt" by them?

HANDOUT 10-3
JOURNAL ABOUT THE LAST TIME I FELT "FELT"

Journal Prompts:

- Who do you feel knows you?
- List some times when you felt "felt."
- By whom did you or do you feel "felt"?
- What did they do that fostered this feeling in you?
- What was it like for you to "feel felt"?
- What did you notice about your emotions when you felt "felt"?
- List some times when you did not feel "felt."
- Why did you feel this way?
- What could have been done differently to help you feel "felt"?
- Identify the emotions that arose when you didn't feel "felt."
- Who might feel "felt" by you?
- What can you do differently to improve how others feel "felt" by you?
- Is there anything you can do to feel "felt" by others?

Chapter 11: Mindfulness of Tasks

Tool 11-1: Mindfulness During Daily Activity

THEORY: One aspect of mindfulness involves being mindful of doing tasks while doing the tasks. This differs from more formal sitting mindfulness meditations in that it is a skill that can be incorporated into the daily routine, while doing tasks or activities, no matter what the task. Practicing mindfulness while engaged in daily activities helps with concentration (and therefore, memory), efficiency, and stress. This tool introduces the concept of being mindful while doing any task.

IMPLEMENTATION: Explain to your client that mindfulness of tasks simply means to pay attention to what they are doing while they are doing it. As soon as they notice that their mind has wandered (that's normal), gently return their attention to the task at hand. Describe how they can practice this skill no matter what they are doing during the day. Some examples are while driving, eating, taking a shower, going for a walk, doing homework or a work project, washing the dishes, getting ready for bed, and making love. Ask the client to close their eyes and imagine they are brushing their teeth. Read Handout 11-1 to them. Then ask them to pick a few tasks they routinely perform during each day and use this technique to practice being mindful while doing them.

PROCESSING: Help your client reflect on what it was like to pay such close attention to every detail of a task such as brushing their teeth. Did their mind wander? Tell them that with 60,000 thoughts a day it's perfectly normal for their mind to wander. Were they able to notice that it wandered and bring their attention back to the task? Ask them what task they practiced being mindful of. What did they notice about their ability to pay attention? Did they do a better job while being mindful? Was it easier to remember what they did? Was their mind calmer as it turned off the busy distracting chatter while they practiced being present? Did they notice any change in their stress level, anxiety, or feelings of being overwhelmed?

HANDOUT 11-1
MINDFULNESS DURING DAILY ACTIVITY

No matter what task you are doing, you can be more present and aware of the moment by practicing mindfulness of tasks. Simply pay attention to what you are doing. As soon as you notice that your attention has wandered, gently return it to the task at hand. Repeat this process until the task it done.

Here's an example. Use this process no matter what task you are engaged in.

Mindfulness While Brushing Your Teeth

- Stand in front of the bathroom sink.

- Look at yourself in the mirror and slowly take a deep belly breath and sigh as you exhale.

- Pick up your toothbrush from wherever it lives.

- As you grasp the handle of the toothbrush, pay attention to how it feels in your hand. Is it hard, squishy, warm, cold, sticky, smooth, or textured?

- Now put the toothbrush under the faucet and turn on the water.

- As you do so, notice how the faucet handle feels on your fingers. Is it cool, hot, slippery, smooth, or sticky? Is it shiny or dull? Is it covered with drops of water?

- As the water starts to run into the sink, look at it for a moment. What does it look like? Is it a steady stream? Is it frothy? Is it dripping or rushing out? Is it going quickly down the drain or starting to fill up the sink?

- Place your toothbrush under the water and notice how your hand feels as the water flows over the toothbrush. Did your hand get wet? What sound do you notice with the water running?

- Pick up the toothpaste container. Notice how much it weighs. Pay attention to how it feels in your hand. Is it warm, cold, smooth, rough, sticky? Is it hard, stiff, or flexible?

- Open the toothpaste container and smell the toothpaste. What do you notice about the fragrance? Is it a fresh smell? Is it minty or some other flavor?

- Notice how your hand feels on the toothpaste container as you put some toothpaste on your brush. Pay attention to the toothpaste as it glides onto the brush. What color is it? Can you smell it?

- Notice how your mouth feels as you put the toothbrush into your mouth and start to brush your teeth. Is there a tingling sensation from the toothpaste? Is your mouth full of froth? How do the bristles feel on your teeth? How about on your gums or your tongue?

- Now notice how your mouth feels as you rinse it out with water. Run your tongue around your teeth. Do they feel clean, smooth, sharp, jagged, bumpy, or slippery?

- Pay attention to how the brush looks as you rinse it with water.

- Notice how your hand feels as you put the brush and the toothpaste away.

- Look at yourself in the mirror.

- Take a deep cleansing breath and give yourself a big smile.

Tool 11-2: Mindfulness of Tasks

THEORY: One of the easiest and most basic forms of mindfulness is practicing mindfulness while doing a task or activity. Mindfulness of tasks simply involves deciding to focus your attention on all aspects of the task at hand, noticing when your mind wanders, and bringing your attention back to the task. It entails noticing every little detail of what you are doing and involves as many of your senses as possible including sight, sound, touch, smell, and if appropriate, taste.

IMPLEMENTATION: Review the concept of mindfulness of tasks. Ask the client to close their eyes and listen while you read the Mindfulness of Driving meditation in Handout 11-2 to them. Then encourage them to use this skill when they are doing tasks during the week and tell you about their experience next session.

PROCESSING: Guide the client to reflect on what it feels like to be mindful while doing tasks. Ask them what happened when they did it. What did they notice about their concentration, emotions, energy? How did they bring their attention back when it wandered? Did they feel more efficient? Did their busy mind calm down?

HANDOUT 11-2
MINDFULNESS OF DRIVING

One of the easiest and most basic forms of mindfulness is practicing mindfulness while doing a task or activity. Mindfulness of tasks simply involves deciding to focus your attention on all aspects of the task at hand, noticing when your mind wanders, and bringing your attention back to the task. It entails noticing every little detail of what you are doing and involves as many of your senses as possible including sight, sound, touch, smell, and if appropriate, taste.

Here's an example to practice while you are driving. You can apply this process to any task such as eating, taking a shower, cleaning house, working on a project, doing a work or school assignment, making love, going for a walk, and so on.

When you are driving, it is easy to get into "automatic" mode. How often have you driven someplace and when you arrive you have no memory of going past certain landmarks or turning onto certain roads? Driving is sometimes done using our subconscious ability without much conscious thought.

Here's how to drive mindfully. Before you get into the car, look at the outside of the car and notice the color, style, whether it's dirty or clean, shiny, dull, whether it's your favorite kind of car or one you want to trade in. When you get into the car, notice how you feel as you slide into the driver's seat. Is it comfortable, familiar, or uncomfortable? Is the inside of the car neat and clean or does it need some attention later?

As you are sitting in the driver's seat, notice the feel of the steering wheel as you grasp it with your hands and fingers. Is it warm, cold, hard, soft, smooth, slippery, or sticky? Notice how the seat feels against your back and bottom. Is it soft, hard, cushiony? Pay attention as you put the key in the ignition and start the car. Does the key slide in effortlessly or take some fiddling to get it working? How does the car sound? Does it have a nice hum, a roar? Is it running smoothly or misfiring?

As you check the mirrors and drive the car out of its parking spot, look out the window and notice what you see there. Do you see other cars? Is there a lot of traffic? What type of road are you driving on? Pay attention to the other cars as they come into your view, as they go by going the other direction, as they travel beside you on a highway. Check the rearview and side mirrors quickly and keep your eyes on the road. Notice the cars, pedestrians, bicycles, or anything else that is sharing the road or might be pulling onto the road. Be alert for anything that requires you to change speed or direction.

Every time you realize that your thoughts are wandering, just acknowledge it and return your attention to driving. You might repeat the words "driving, driving" to help you stay focused. Notice the traffic signs, the traffic lights, and the markings on the road. Notice the cars that are close to you. Notice the scenery or the buildings as you drive by them. Keep your eyes on the road. Bring your awareness back to the feel of the steering wheel. Notice how it feels now that you have been holding onto it for a while. Repeat "driving, driving." Notice how your foot feels on the accelerator. Is it easy to push down, does it push back against your foot? If you are shifting, how does the clutch feel on your left foot and the gas pedal on your right? How does the shifter feel against your hand? Be conscious of changing gears. Notice how the engine sounds change as the gears shift. Check the mirrors and keep your eyes on the road and your awareness on the task of driving until you arrive at your destination.

Reflect on the experience of being mindful while driving. Do you remember more of the trip? Are there any parts of the trip you don't remember? Is your mind clearer than usual? Do you have more energy? How far did you get before you realized you weren't thinking about driving? What worked best to get your attention back on driving?

Tool 11-3: Journal About Increasing Mindfulness of Tasks

THEORY: Being mindful while performing tasks may be a new concept for most clients. Encourage them to journal about their experience as they practice this skill.

IMPLEMENTATION: Ask the client to respond to the journal prompts in Handout 11-3 either in writing or verbally. Explain the goal of this exercise is to help them reflect on their experience with mindfulness of tasks practice and help them integrate it into their life as well as refine their skill.

PROCESSING: Review the client's answers to the journal prompts with them. Process their experience with Mindfulness of Tasks. Explore what arose for them during the practice and during the journaling about the practice.

HANDOUT 11-3
JOURNAL ABOUT INCREASING MINDFULNESS OF TASKS

Journal Prompts:

- What tasks have you done while practicing mindfulness of tasks?
- Were you able to stay focused?
- What distracted you?
- How did you bring your attention back to the task?
- What did you notice inside you when practicing this skill?
- Did it take more or less time than usual to complete the task?
- Did you make mistakes while doing the task?
- Did you feel more or less stressed than usual?
- Did you notice anything new about this task?
- Did this practice help you calm your busy brain?
- Have you ever done something that you can't remember doing afterwards such as putting something someplace, or driving by a landmark, or shaving?
- Do you find it easier to remember when you use mindfulness?
- What tasks might be done better if you were being more mindful?
- If you were having surgery, would you like to know that your surgeon was mindful?
- Draw a picture of yourself being mindful while doing a task.

Chapter 12: Mindfulness of Words

Tool 12-1: One Word at a Time

THEORY: A basic skill of mindfulness practice is to be able to notice, accept, and dismiss distracting thoughts, body sensations, and sounds in the environment. This tool provides a fun way to strengthen the process of letting go of thoughts and emotions that are triggered by words. It also provides an opportunity to explore what thoughts or emotions were triggered during the practice.

IMPLEMENTATION: Explain to your client that you are going to do an exercise with them that strengthens their ability to notice, accept, and dismiss thoughts while being mindful. Explain that this exercise will give them confidence that they CAN observe without getting stuck on or reacting to what they observe—a basic component of mindfulness.

Read the One Word at a Time exercise in Handout 12-1. You can replace the words on the list with any words you feel appropriate for your client. Throw in some "off-the-wall" words to try and get the clients to react such as donkey snot, nose hair, piggy bank, tutu, etc. Include a variety of words that might evoke various emotional responses.

PROCESSING: Invite your client to talk about what happened. Ask them, "Did you have any thoughts, urges, sensations, images, emotions that arose when you heard any particular word?" Explore what the client experienced. Ask them to notice if they were able to observe all the things brought up in their mind and body by the words without getting "stuck." Were they able to let go and move on to the next word? Explain that they can practice this process any time to increase mindfulness of the present just as they did with the exercise.

Some clients will have strong reactions to some of the words. If it's appropriate, explore what came up for the client. This often provides an opening for doing some great therapeutic work albeit not specifically mindfulness.

HANDOUT 12-1
ONE WORD AT A TIME

Find yourself a comfortable position with your feet flat on the floor, back resting against the back of the chair, arms resting gently in your lap with palms facing up.

When you are ready, close your eyes. Now take a deep breath in through your nose and out through your mouth. Do it again. With each breath relax and clear out your mind more and more. One more time. Inhale awareness, and exhale distraction.

Tune in to my voice. I am going to say a set of words one at a time. I will say one word and then pause for a moment. Then I will say another word and pause for another moment and so on and so forth. Your task is to notice what comes up in you when I say a word, such as a thought, feeling, urge, image, or physical sensation. Go with me from word to word to word. At the end I will invite you to open your eyes and return your attention to the room.

Fun, breakfast, calendar, awareness, love, relationship, war, peace, nose hair, lavender, hammock, dog drool, mindfulness, kitten, sleep, exercise, healing.*

Open your eyes and come on back to the room when you are ready.

*You can replace the words on the list with any words you feel appropriate for your client. Make it fun.

Tool 12-2: Telling Your Story

THEORY: Words are extremely powerful. Most of us are not aware of the words we use on a regular basis, nor why we use them. We tell the stories about our life in many different ways. Some tell a story of woe, victimization, trauma while others describe similar events with hope, pride of accomplishment, and overcoming obstacles.

This exercise is designed to increase awareness of words that are used and to increase understanding of why they are being chosen. It is aimed at increasing the ability to remain mindful when speaking. It opens the door for change.

IMPLEMENTATION: Ask your client to tell you a story about something that happened in their life. Tell them to include how they felt about it. It can be a funny story, or something that was difficult, or something they can never forget, or even just something that happened yesterday that they would like to share. Explain that you will be listening carefully to their story and that you will be writing down some of the words they use as they speak. Tell them to ignore when you write and stay focused on their story. Tell them to keep in mind that you will stop them in 2 minutes if they haven't finished already.

Now listen carefully and write down some of the themes of their story. Pay particular attention to the actual words they use.

Here's an example of what you might discover. You may find patterns of words that exaggerate, or words with negative or positive feelings associated with them. The words may describe action or various types of emotion. They may be blaming, hopeful, critical, encouraging, or judgmental. They may be descriptive, factual, interpretative, or reactive. Just tune into the story and write down words that pop out at you for any reason or that are repeated.

Stop the client at 2 minutes and review the words that you wrote down with your client.

After reviewing the words as described in the Processing section, then teach your client that in order to increase mindfulness of words they can practice being aware of the words being used. Ask them to tune into their own conversations and the words they use for a few minutes at a time. Explain that when they are more mindful of the words they choose, they have more opportunity to choose words that align more closely with their intention or the story they would really like to be telling versus the old story that may or may not be working for them.

PROCESSING: Help the client clarify what they meant when they used certain words. Look for patterns, meaning, and how they interpreted what happened in their story. Help the client determine if there is a consistency between the words they use and the story they would really like to tell. Explore what happened when they tuned into their own conversations. What words did they notice? Were they surprised by the words they chose? Were the words consistent with how they see themselves?

Chapter 13: Mindfulness of Intention

Tool 13-1: Explore Your True Intentions

THEORY: Setting an intention is a first step in any activity or discipline. In setting an intention we decide what we intend to pay attention to. Doing so helps us stay focused on a specific goal or task. In mindfulness we must set an intention every time we practice. For example in the Awareness of Breath Mindfulness Tool 5-5 we must first set an intention to pay attention to our breath. In the Mindfulness of Tasks Tool 11-1 we set an intention to pay attention to the task at hand. This tool provides a structured method for defining our intention and clarifying why we set that particular intention and what we hope to gain from achieving it.

IMPLEMENTATION: Explain to clients that this exercise provides them with a structured way to define and support any intention they may have. Ask clients to complete the sentences provided in Handout 13-1 using mindfulness to fill in the blanks. Explain that this process will help them clarify their own intention of becoming more mindful. It will help them explore why they want to increase mindfulness in their life and how they hope it will improve their life. Remind them that they can use this process for any intention or goal.

PROCESSING: Help your client reflect on what this process was like for them. Ask them: Did any of your answers surprise you? What thoughts or emotions came up for you? Were your able to clarify your intention? Were any of the questions difficult to answer? How will you remind yourself that you set this intention and get back on track if you get side-tracked? What other intentions might you use this process to clarify?

HANDOUT 13-1
EXPLORE YOUR TRUE INTENTIONS

This sentence-completion exercise will help you begin to get in touch with your true intentions. The following example is designed to explore the intentions behind practicing mindfulness. Simply replace the word "mindfulness" with any intention that you wish to explore:

- I want to learn about (mindfulness) because . . .
- I am hoping that (mindfulness) will give me . . .
- (Mindfulness) is . . .
- If I am more (mindful), then I will . . .
- The real reasons that I want to (practice mindfulness) are . . .
- Ultimately, (mindfulness) will allow me to . . .
- When I (practice mindfulness), it makes me feel . . .

Be as honest as possible when completing the sentences.

Use this process with any part of your life to help you discover your true intentions. Then set your intention, monitor your progress, and repeatedly check in to be mindful of your intention and adjust your thoughts and actions as necessary to stay on course.

Adapted from (Alidina, 2011).

Tool 13-2: Meditation

THEORY: Visualization and imagining are a great way to "practice" anything we want to improve our ability to accomplish. This tool provides a way to practice setting an intention and staying focused on that intention. It helps the client visualize what a mindful day might look like to help them understand how they can incorporate mindfulness into their day.

IMPLEMENTATION: Explain that an important step in becoming more mindful is to practice setting an intention to do so and then to follow through on that intention. Explain that the purpose of the Intention to Be Mindful Meditation in Handout 13-2 is to help them imagine that they have set an intention to be mindful and that they are following through on that intention throughout the day. It illustrates how to set and follow through on intention as well as how to incorporate mindfulness into their day. Read the meditation to the client. Encourage them to set their own intention to become more mindful and practice doing so during their day.

PROCESSING: Explore what came up for the client during the meditation. Discuss their intention to be more mindful. Compare how they would incorporate mindfulness in their day to the suggestions in the meditation. Explore what gets in their way of following through on their intention. See Tool 4-7 for options for dealing with obstacles and resistance.

HANDOUT 13-2
INTENTION TO BE MINDFUL MEDITATION

Close your eyes and take a nice slow breath in through your nose to the count of four. 1-2-3-4. Now exhale slowly through your mouth like you are blowing a bubble to the count of eight. 1-2-3-4-5-6-7-8. Now relax and breath normally.

Now imagine that you have set an intention to be more mindful throughout your day. Picture yourself getting ready in the morning. Pay attention to each of the tasks you routinely do such as brushing your teeth, taking a shower, getting dressed, and eating breakfast. Imagine that as you do each task you are fully present in that moment. You are paying attention to the task. When your mind wanders and starts to think about something other than what you are doing, you remember your intention, notice the thought, let it go, and bring your attention back to the task at hand.

Notice as you go through the activities of the day that you are focusing on staying mindful along the way—just as you intended to do. You notice everything about the car or bus, and the road and the scenery as you drive or ride to work or school. You enjoy the beautiful sky. You notice the leaves, flowers, trees, or perhaps the snow along the way.

When you arrive, you notice your surroundings when you first walk in and get settled for the day. You make eye contact with those you meet during the day. You pay close attention to the other person in all your conversations and you truly listen to them without allowing your mind to be distracted.

While you are working on each task, you stay focused on that task. Whenever your mind wanders, you gently bring it back to the task. You remind yourself of your intention to be mindful today.

Whenever you feel hurried, stressed, or overwhelmed, you stop, take a belly breath, bring your awareness to your inner landscape, put things in perspective, and then mindfully choose how to respond or to approach the next task. You remember your intention.

When you interact with others, you bring your full attention to them. You make eye contact. You listen carefully to what they say. When you notice your mind is wandering, you gently refocus on the person you are talking with.

At lunch time you take a break from work or school. You carefully choose healthy foods and eat mindfully noticing everything about the smell, feel, and taste of your food. You pay attention to feeling full.

You take advantage of the time you already set aside to practice a mindfulness exercise or meditation. You listen to a guided meditation or you practice Awareness of Breath or any of a number of different exercises you have learned.

You get some exercise. No matter how you work out, you remind yourself of your intention and you practice being mindful of every aspect of the physical sensations of exercising and of your surroundings.

Later, when you arrive home, you shift your attention to your surroundings and to home life. When thoughts of work arise, notice them, let them go, and return your focus to your home and those you live with and the activities of home life.

At bedtime, you focus on all aspects of getting ready for bed including turning the lights down low, saying goodnight to loved ones, doing your nighttime routine, and climbing into bed. You are mindful of how good the bed feels and of how tired you are.

You spend a few moments reviewing all the things that happened today that you are grateful for. You realize how calm and grounded you felt all day. You notice that your emotional landscape was well regulated and on an even keel all day despite triggers that might have set you off. You look back on your accomplishments of the day and discover that you completed more tasks with much less effort. You are glad that you decided to intend to be more mindful.

You practice a short mindfulness meditation in bed to prepare yourself for restful, rejuvenating sleep.

The next morning you wake up refreshed and energized.

Chapter 14: Mindfulness of Intuition

Tool 14-1: Tuning-In

THEORY: An important aspect of mindfulness is the ability to tune in to our intuition, our inner wisdom. An intuition often shows up as a "gut feeling" about something that you find out later was completely accurate. This Mindfulness of Intuition Tool explains intuition and strengthens the ability to tune in and more accurately interpret and trust it.

IMPLEMENTATION: Use the handout to discuss the definition of intuition with your clients and explore what they think it is. Review the process of developing intuition as described in Handout 14-1A with them. Use Handout 14-1B to help them explore how their intuition works.

PROCESSING: Discuss what role intuition plays in your client's life. Explore how your client tunes into their intuition. Discuss how their intuition gives them information, for example, via a physical sensation, through a dream, just a knowing. Examine how they can tap into their intuition more routinely.

HANDOUT 14-1A
TUNING INTO INTUITION

There are many different definitions of intuition:

- The direct perception of truth or fact that is independent of any reasoning process or previous knowledge

- The ability to have a quick and accurate insight about something

- The appearance in the mind of accurate information about the external world, which can be shown to have come not through the five senses, nor through a rearrangement of stored memory contents (Bernstein, 2005)

- Write your definition here:

_____

_____

_____

_____

There are various ways intuition can guide us:

- As a "feeling" about someone we just met or about something we are about to do, or about a decision we are trying to make.

- As "information" that we have no way of logically knowing. We just feel it or know it.

- As a warning of danger.

- How has intuition helped you?

Intuition may show up as:

- A physical sensation

- A "gut feeling"

- A knowing

- A hunch

- A dream

- How does your intuition show up for you?

Intuition happens:

- Instantaneously, in a fraction of a second

- Repeatedly until we "get it"

In order to develop your intuition, you must first make the decision to focus on it and study how it shows up for you. You must learn to understand the "language" of how your intuition works. Intuition can come in the form of feelings, emotions, a knowing, and hunches. It may show up in the words you hear from others. It may use symbols to communicate with you. It may come through dreams.

Think about how your intuition works. Fantasize, visualize, and use your imagination. Find a quiet place, clear your mind, and go inside yourself. Ask for answers to questions or decisions you need help with. Be patient. Feed your intuition the information you have about something you need help with and then let it simmer in your subconscious. Look for signs of the intuitive answers. Keep a daily journal of what you need answers for and what shows up during your day. Make sure to express gratitude when you get your answers. And keep a dream journal to help understand how your dreams are giving you guidance.

Meditate to get more in touch with your intuition. By meditating, you calm your busy mind and allow your intuition to flow more easily. Meditation helps you and your rational mind get out of the way. Ask for answers or guidance and then be still and quiet and listen for what shows up.

Study your intuitions. Learn how your intuition works best. Pay attention to which "hunches" were the most accurate. Figure out in what areas your intuition works best for you and trust it when your experience has shown you it's most likely to be accurate. For example, maybe you are always right about people, but not about which line to get in at the store.

Play with it. Have fun. You intuition is always operating whether or not you are tuned into it. You will be amazed to discover just how much you use it already.

Tool 14-2: Mindfulness of Intuition Meditation

THEORY: One effective way to tune into intuition is to practice a meditation that helps you connect to your inner wisdom or intuition. This tool provides an example of a guided meditation that first helps you relax and open up to communication with your inner wisdom.

IMPLEMENTATION: Discuss intuition with your client—what it is, why it is important, how it can be helpful, how it can show up. See Tool 14-1. Explain that the Mindfulness of Intuition Meditation is designed to help them open up the communication and tune in to their own intuition. Read the meditation in Handout 14-2 to your client.

PROCESSING: Discuss what came up for your client during the meditation. Were they able to relax? Did they have a question for the white board? Did they get an answer? Did the white board draw a picture or use words to communicate? What did they do to stay focused? What thoughts, feelings, mental pictures, body sensations, smells, sounds, colors, or memories arose? Did they feel like they got a message from within? Have they heard this message before?

HANDOUT 14-2
MINFULNESS OF INTUITION MEDITATION

Find yourself a comfortable position sitting upright in a chair with your feet flat on the floor, legs uncrossed, back resting gently against the back of the chair, arms unfolded resting lightly on your thighs, with palms facing up. Take a deep cleansing breathe in through your nose to the count of four. Exhale through your mouth to the count of eight and as you exhale relax your mind. Take another deep breath and inhale healing energy and as you exhale relax your body. Now allow your breath to be effortless and automatic.

Take a few moments to relax your body. Start by focusing on your toes. Notice what's there. Fill your toes with warmth and loving kindness. Then focus on your legs including your calves and shins, knees, thighs. Again just notice what's there and send gentle and loving thoughts to your legs. Now focus on your bottom. Notice any tension that may be stored here and let it go. You just don't need it. Let it flow down your thighs, through your knees, through your calves and shins to your feet, right through the ends of your toes and onto the floor. Now bring your awareness to your abdomen and stomach area. Again, just notice what's there and allow anything that needs to go to flow out with every breath. Now pay attention to your back including your lower back, mid-back, upper back, and shoulders. Lots of stuff gets carried here and you just don't need any of it. Let it flow down through your bottom, through your legs, through your feet, right through the ends of your toes and onto the floor.

Now focus on your chest area including your lungs and heart. Intentionally inhale and fill your lungs with a cushion of healing energy. As you exhale, release anything that needs to go. Imagine you are breathing in through your heart. As you do this, imagine a feeling of appreciation or gratitude. Allow this feeling to flow into your heart and from there throughout the rest of your body. Now focus on your arms and hands. Notice what's there and let go of anything that needs to go. Let it flow from your shoulders down your upper arms, your elbows, your wrists, your hands, and right through the ends of your fingers and onto the floor. Now pay attention to your neck and throat. Inhale and fill this area with healing energy and feel a gentle release as your exhale. Now place your tongue on the bottom of your mouth behind your teeth and relax your jaw. Let it drop and hang down, totally relaxed. Raise your focus to your face including your cheeks, your eyes, and your forehead. Tighten all these muscles. Scrunch them up, tight, tight, tight. Then release the tension. Feel the difference between tense and relaxed. Now focus on your scalp from your forehead and ears all the way up and over and down to the base of your scalp at your neck. Again, just notice what's there and let go of anything that needs to go. Now take a deep cleansing breath and fill your entire body and head with a cushion of healing energy. As you exhale, let go of anything that still needs to go. Let go of it. You just don't need it.

Now imagine a white light shining down from above into the crown of your head, filling your head and body with healing energy, going down your neck and throat and down your spine vertebrae by vertebrae. As it flows down, it shines out in front of you as far as you can see and out behind you and beside you as far as you can see. It flows down through your legs and right through the bottoms of your feet into the earth. As it fills you, it warms, cleanses, clears, and heals. It connects you to the universe and to the earth all at the same time. It connects the within with the without, and with creation.

As your body is enjoying this peaceful, relaxed feeling, imagine that you are walking along a path. You come to a garden gate which has been left open for you. You enter the garden, close the gate behind you, and find a comfortable place to sit down amongst the beauty and peace of the garden. You close your eyes and go within.

You set your intention to connect with and communicate with your intuition. You focus your awareness on what arises from this calm, quiet place inside you. You might imagine a blank white board in front of you. If you have a question you need answered, write it on the board and wait for an answer. If you don't have a question, just sit quietly. In either case pay attention to any thoughts, feelings, mental pictures, body sensations, smells, sounds, colors, or memories that arise. Allow contact with your inner knowing. Tune in. Notice if anything gets written on the board for you. Ask for guidance if you want it. Ask for signs that help you connect with inner wisdom and intuition. Then relax and wait. Just be. If your mind wanders, just bring it back to your intention to connect with your intuition.

Wait patiently, watch, and listen. Stay alert to what is presenting itself to you. Pay attention and trust that you are receiving exactly what you need to know right now.

2-Minute Silence (Note: Vary length of this silent period as appropriate.)

Now that you have connected with your intuition and received important messages and guidance, be grateful that you are getting better and better about being mindful of your intuition. Slowly stand up in the garden and walk quietly toward the gate. Open it, walk through, and leave it open as you found it. Walk along the path and return to this room, bringing the peace and wisdom you found in the garden with you. You can open your eyes when you are ready.

Tool 14-3: Journal About Mindfulness of Intuition

THEORY: Being able to tap into intuition appears to be an innate skill, but it is often ignored. Journaling about how intuition displays itself and how to tune into it more effectively will help the client be increasingly aware of intuitive messages and to learn to trust them.

IMPLEMENTATION: Ask your client to answer the journal prompts in Handout 14-3.

PROCESSING: Review your client's answers and process what came up for them during their journaling. Explore how intuition plays a role in their life. Examine how their intuition communicates with them. Discuss how the Mindfulness of Intuition tools have increased their ability to tune in to their intuition.

HANDOUT 14-3
JOURNAL ABOUT MINDFULNESS OF INTUITION

Journal Prompts:

- What role has intuition played in your life?
- Give some examples of when your intuition was accurate.
- Is there anything your intuition has been wrong about?
- When did you follow your intuition?
- What happened when you followed it?
- When did you ignore your intuition?
- What happened when you ignored it?
- What helps you tune into your intuition?
- How does your intuition communicate with you?
- Do you trust it?
- What would help you trust it more?
- What does your intuition help you with the most?
- Does your intuition communicate through dreams?
- Have you tried keeping a dream journal and if so how did that help you?

Chapter 15: Mindfulness of Motion

Tool 15-1: Motion

THEORY: Many people have difficulty sitting still for very long especially if they have ADHD, anxiety, or pain. This Mindfulness of Motion tool provides a way for these people to practice mindfulness while helping to overcome the obstacle presented by their difficulty sitting still. It can be substituted for sitting meditations to provide more variety.

IMPLEMENTATION: Using Handout 15-1 as a guide, lead your client through the motions while modeling the movements for them. Remind them to pay attention to how their body feels as they move. Modify the motions as needed for particular clients. Expand this exercise to dancing. Try these exercises while listening to music or drumming. Ask your client to notice where they feel the music in their body.

PROCESSING: Ask your client to reflect on how their body moved with the various motions. Discuss what they noticed about their body as they moved. How did their body feel differently with the different movements? What were they thinking about while they were moving? How did they handle distractions? Was it easier stay focused while moving or while being still?

HANDOUT 15-1
MINDFULNESS OF MOTION MEDITATION

Let's do a Mindfulness of Motion meditation. Sit down and close your eyes. Sit up straight with your feet flat on the floor and your hands resting in your lap. Now lean to the right. Notice how your body feels as you shift your weight. How does your right hip feel different from your left hip? Do you feel a stretch on your left hip and waist? Now move slowly back to the center, pause there, and then lean to the left. Notice how your body feels here. Notice what has changed in your left hip as it takes more weight. How does your right hip feel different?

Now, slowly rock back and forth. Notice the sensations in your body. Keep rocking. Pay attention to how your bottom feels on the chair. What are your feet doing? How is your head handling the movement? Are you feeling dizzy? Where are you looking?

Now stand up straight with your arms at your sides. Notice how your shoulders feel as your hands hang beside you. Notice how your feet feel carrying your weight.

Now push your hands straight up above your head and straighten your arms. Notice the sensation in your arms as you raise them and straighten them. Do you feel a stretch? Are they tight, relaxed, comfortable, or uncomfortable? Bring them down to your shoulders. How do they feel now?

Push them up and down like you are lifting a barbell. Notice what changes as you repeat this motion.

Now bring your arms down to your side. Lean to your right and put your weight on your right foot. What do you notice about how your right foot feels? How about your left foot? Now lean back to the center and pause. Notice how the sensations in your feet and legs and body have changed. Now lean to the left and again be mindful of how your feet, legs, hips, back, shoulder, arms, and neck feel as they move.

Now, gently rock back and forth from left to right and right to left. Keep rocking while you pay attention to how your body feels as it rocks. Go slowly, then quickly. Rock wide, then narrow. Keep noticing how your body feels and how it changes as you move.

Now come back to center. Bring you right arm in front of your tummy and your left arm behind your back. Notice how your arms feel. Now reverse this and bring your right arm behind you and your left arm in front. Again notice the feeling. Now swing them back and forth in these positions from front to back and vice versa. Enjoy the rhythm of the motion as your arms swing from front to back and let them touch your belly and back as they stop and turn around. What do you notice as you do this for a little while? Does anything change? Do the motions seem easier, harder, soothing, or jarring?

Now stop your arms and bring them back to your sides, noticing how this change feels. And slowly sit down while paying attention to how it feels to sit and put your weight back on your bottom.

Tool 15-2: Stillness

THEORY: Being able to sit still and experience complete stillness is a novelty for many clients, but an important mindfulness skill. This tool leads the client in a brief meditation to experience stillness while observing and not reacting.

IMPLEMENTATION: Explain that one component of mindfulness is being able to sit and experience stillness of the body and mind. Use Handout 15-2 to lead clients through a brief meditation to help them practice stillness.

PROCESSING: Help clients explore what this meditation was like for them. Did they have trouble sitting still? Did they feel the need or urge to scratch an itch? How did they resist urges to move? What did they notice about their body in the stillness? What thoughts arose? Did they experience any emotions? Did they find this meditation calming? Did they feel restless? Did it get harder or easier to maintain stillness with time?

HANDOUT 15-2
STILLNESS

Let's practice tuning in to stillness in the mind and body.

You may do this meditation in any position in which you feel most comfortable. Settle into the position. Close your eyes and take a deep belly breath in through your nose and out through your mouth like you are slowly blowing a bubble. Then simply breathe normally without changing it.

Imagine that someone has sprinkled you with freeze dust and notice how it feels as your body becomes totally still. Notice as everything slowly settles down. Sit with this feeling of stillness. Notice your breath. Become aware of the urges and sensations in your body. If you feel an itch, just notice it, and let it go by focusing your attention on another part of your body that isn't itchy. If you feel the urge to shift and move your arm or leg, again, just notice the urge, let it go, and focus your attention on another part of your body that feels comfortable. If you notice a thought that is not about this stillness, acknowledge it, accept it, and let it go. Return you attention to your stillness.

Imagine your mind is settling and calming as your body does the same. Notice that as you experience this stillness, you begin to feel quiet, calm, almost as if you are floating. Remember to breathe. Fill your body with a cushion of healing energy. If any body part becomes uncomfortable, inhale and fill that part of your body with a cushion of air. As you exhale, let go of everything that needs to go.

Continue this process and sit in this stillness for 2 minutes. (Vary this time as appropriate.)

Tool 15-3: Slow Walking Meditation

THEORY: Walking meditation is a great alternative to sitting meditation. It helps clients focus on their bodily sensations as they walk slowly and deliberately. Walking meditation is a contemplative practice where close attention is paid to the action of walking. It is not thinking or contemplating about some topic while walking (that's a different form of walking meditation). It is being mindful of the muscles of your body, the placement of your feet, balance, and motion. Walking meditation has a long tradition in Buddhism. It can be practiced anywhere. It can also be practiced while walking a labyrinth.

IMPLEMENTATION: Explain to your client that Walking Meditation is a contemplative practice that includes paying attention to every detail of the motion of walking. Take your client to a place where they have room to walk at least 20 to 30 steps. Then read the Slow Walking Meditation in Handout 15-3 to them as they follow the instructions. Do it with them. Encourage them to practice this technique whenever they walk, even if it's just every time they walk to the restroom.

PROCESSING: Explore what the Slow Walking Meditation was like for the client. Was it difficult to walk so slowly? Did they stay focused and, if not, what distracted them? How did they get refocused on the task of walking? What did they notice about their body as they walked? Did their mind feel more calm? Did their busy brain quiet down? Were they able to stay present?

HANDOUT 15-3
SLOW WALKING MEDITATION

Walking Meditation Practice

In walking meditation, we focus on the movement of each step and on the body as we move. Since walking is part of our daily lives, walking meditation is a great way to increase and practice mindfulness. You can do it anywhere and anytime you walk. It can help you feel connected to the earth and fully present in your body. It can help you calm the busy chatter of your mind and allow a clearer presence. For this exercise, find a place where you have room to walk back and forth, at least 10 to 20 steps in length. You can practice inside or when you go for a walk outside or on a treadmill. Keep your hands still, either behind your back, or at your sides.

Notice your breath for a moment as it flows effortlessly in and out. Stand and balance your weight evenly between both feet. Now feel the sensations of standing. Bring your attention to your body. Be conscious of contact with the ground, of pressure and tension.

Pay attention to how it feels to stand.

Notice how all the parts of your body participate in standing including your feet, ankles, legs, hips, stomach, chest, back, shoulders, and arms.

Now lean gently to the left.

Notice what feels different as you put all your weight on your left foot. Pay attention to the feeling in your left foot, leg, hip and your back, neck, and arms. Pay attention to the feeling in your right foot, leg, and hip. Notice the difference between the sensations in the two sides of your body.

Now lean to the right.

Notice how your body changes as your weight changes. Pay attention to your right foot, leg, hip and then your left foot, leg, and hip.

Slowly and consciously raise your right leg, swing the right foot forward, and step onto it. Put your weight on your right foot and take the weight off your left foot. Notice the sensations in your right foot as it carries your weight. Compare these to the sensations in your left foot as you take your weight off of it.

Slowly and deliberately lift your left foot, swing it forward, and place it on the ground and gently shift your weight onto it.

Repeat this with each foot, being mindful of how each part of your body participates in walking. Notice the sensations in your feet, legs, hips, back, stomach, chest, shoulders, neck, arms and head.

You might say 'lift, swing, and place' as you repeat this process.

Maintain your attention on the process of walking. If your mind wanders, that's okay. As soon as you notice that it has, gently bring your attention back to the action and feeling of walking.

As you walk allow your weight to shift from side to side in a fluid motion. Tune into the motion and the feeling in your body.

You might repeat 'walking, walking' as you slowly walk forward. Turn around if you run out of space.

Now walk more quickly. Maintain the same process of lifting, swinging, and placing. Notice how your body feels now that it is walking faster. How is it different from walking slowly?

Notice the weight of your arms and shoulders as you walk.

The goal is to walk mindfully. Be aware of the sensations of walking. Maintain your attention on all aspects of walking. Notice how your mind begins to quiet and clear.

Walk very slowly again. Then walk briskly. Walk quietly to make no sound like the Indians walked in the woods. Now stomp your feet as you walk. Pay attention to the changing sensations.

Play with different ways to walk. Remember to stay focused on being mindful of walking.

When you are done, take a quick scan of your body. Notice how it feels to be still. Notice the mental clarity of your mind. Enjoy the calmness. Bring the feelings with you as you get back to your day.

Practice Mindful Walking as often as you can as you walk from here to there during your day. Make it a habit to walk mindfully every day by choosing certain times to practice. You might practice on the way to the bathroom or each time you walk to your car or while you are walking for exercise outside or at the gym. Resist the urge to be 'thinking, thinking, thinking' while you walk. Allow the clarity that occurs from choosing to focus on the walking itself.

Tool 15-4: Walking Meditation

THEORY: This tool presents two types of walking meditation. One type of attention is focused on surroundings. The other focuses on contemplation of a particular topic or problem. Both use the process of setting an intention to focus (one on surroundings, one on a particular topic), noticing and dismissing distracting thoughts and feelings, and returning attention to the intended target of attention.

IMPLEMENTATION: Explain to your client that this is a mindfulness skill they can practice anytime they go for a walk. Review the two types of walking meditations in Handout 15-4 with your client and encourage them to try both of them as they go for walks. Go for a walk with them to practice.

PROCESSING: Ask your client when and where they did these walking meditations. Help your client reflect on what these walking meditations were like for them. Which type did they like better? Were they able to stay focused? What distracted them? How do these compare with sitting meditations? Did they notice anything new in their surroundings? How did they feel emotionally and physically when they were done walking? Did they notice a feeling of connectedness or grounding when they practiced the focus of surroundings type? What was it like to pick a topic and stay focused on it? Did they have any insights while doing these?

HANDOUT 15-4
WALKING MEDITATION

Type 1: Focus on Surroundings

Before you start your walk, set your intention to pay attention to your surroundings. If you are walking outside, you might begin by noticing the surface you are walking on and how your feet feel as you walk along. Then look around you. Notice the weather, the temperature, the breeze, the sky, and the clouds. Pay attention to the trees, the leaves, the bark, and branches. Focus on flowers, grass, fields, lakes, or streams. Notice the animals: squirrels, dogs, cats, and birds. Listen to the sounds. Notice the fragrance or odors that you come across. If you are in an urban setting, seek out the natural beauty wherever you find it such as trees planted along sidewalks, flower pots, gardens, and parks. Also, focus on the buildings, the streets, the businesses, the cars, buses, trucks, airplanes, trains, and the people. Notice the colors, the sounds, and the energy around you.

Whenever you notice that you are not thinking about your surroundings, just gently bring your attention back to what you can see around you.

Continue this process until you complete your walk.

Type 2: Contemplative Walking

Choose a topic, idea, concept, or a problem you wish to think about while you are walking. Set your intention to think about it as the target of your attention. Go for your walk. Keep your intended topic in your mind. Every time you notice you are thinking about something else, just accept it and bring your attention back to your intended topic. Be aware of your surroundings for safety. Use your steps to remind you to stay focused as you intended.

Continue this process until you complete your walk.

Chapter 16: Using Sound

Tool 16-1: "AHH" Versus "OM"
Tool 16-2: Music

Tool 16-1: "AHH" Versus "OM"

THEORY: A mantra is a word or phrase that is repeated or chanted during some types of meditation. "OM" and "AHH" are both commonly used as mantras. According to Sri Siva Baba (Baba, 2012), an enlightened Indian master, "AHH" is the sound of creation. The sound "AHH" creates incredible energy of joy, which is creation and healing. Wayne Dyer states that the sound "AHH" "within the name God is the same sound around the world. 'AHH' is found in Allah, Krishna, Jehovah, and Ra for a few examples" (Dyer, 2002). According to the Meditation Society of America (Meditation Society, 2012), the sound "OM" pronounced "a-u-m," is the universal sound and is contained in every word and in everything. When chanting a mantra, your cells all vibrate at the same wavelength as the mantra. Once attuned with this vibration, you connect with everything resonating on that plane of existence. The sound of "OM" is energizing, calming, and healing. This tool introduces these two sounds and gives the client practice using them and comparing them.

IMPLEMENTATION: Explain the theory behind the two sounds, "AHH" and "OM." Ask clients to join you as you inhale and sing "AHH" on the exhale. Do this several times. Then instruct them to keep the sound going. Tell them to take a quick breath whenever they need it. When more than one person is doing so, the sound will continue as long as they don't all breathe at the same time. Ask them to tune into the sound and what they notice inside them while singing "AHH." Now ask them to do the same thing with "OM" instead of "AHH." Explain that they can use either sound to start or end meditations or as a meditation in and of itself.

PROCESSING: Ask clients to explore how they felt while they sang each sound. Did they notice any differences in what arose while doing the two sounds? Which sound did they prefer and why? Discuss how they might incorporate the use of these sounds in their practice.

Tool 16-2: Music

THEORY: Music is often described as the universal language. People from all cultures around the world enjoy and respond to music. Music often evokes similar reactions in people regardless of their background. Mindfulness of Music can be used to help people practice being mindful, in this case by setting the intention to listen to a piece of music and notice everything they can about the music and the experience of listening to it.

IMPLEMENTATION: Play a piece of music and ask clients to listen and notice the style of music, how it feels to listen to it, what they like or don't like about it. You might suggest they stand up and dance with the music. Direct them to notice where they feel the music in their body. Then play a different style of music and ask them to do the same exercise. Vary the music choices so there is a large contrast between the two. For example, play a soothing classical song and then a heavy metal or rock and roll song.

PROCESSING: Ask clients to reflect on their experience listening to the music. What arose in them? What, if any, thoughts, feelings, or memories were triggered by the music? Where did they feel the music in their body? How easy was it to stay focused on the music? What changed in their awareness when the second song was played?

Section IV

Tools for Using Mindfulness Skills for Specific Disorders

Chapter 17: Mood Disorders

DEPRESSION

Tool 17-1: Freedom from Depression in the Moment

THEORY: Mindfulness practice consists of paying attention non-judgmentally to something in particular in the present moment (Kabat-Zinn, 2003). When someone experiences depression, their thoughts tend to be chronically negative and they see everything through a negative filter. This tool provides a technique to increase awareness of the negative thoughts and to shift focus to the something that feels better in the present moment.

IMPLEMENTATION: If your client is depressed, ask them to pay attention to the content of their thoughts to discover if they are chronically negative. Explain how negative thoughts lead to negative feelings and ask them if this happens for them. Tell them this mindfulness skill will give them a technique they can use anytime they notice they feel depressed to change their pattern of negative thoughts and shift their mood to a more neutral or positive feeling. When repeated over and over again, this process will slowly rewire the brain to automatically think more positive thoughts. Use Handout 17-1 to lead the client through the "Freedom from Depression in the Moment" meditation.

PROCESSING: Guide your client to reflect on what they noticed while doing this meditation. Did they notice thoughts? Were they negative? If so, were they able to inflate and burst them? Did the negative thoughts recur? Were they able to think of something more pleasant? How did focusing on something in their surroundings feel? What did they notice about their mood? How did it change as they did the meditation? Encourage them to utilize this process anytime they feel depressed.

HANDOUT 17-1
FREEDOM FROM DEPRESSION IN THE MOMENT

Find yourself a comfortable position and take a deep breath in through your nose to the count of four, 1-2-3-4, and exhale slowly through your mouth to the count of eight as if you are blowing a bubble. 1-2-3-4-5-6-7-8.

Now breathe normally and allow your breath to flow in and out of you effortlessly without attempting to change it. Let it flow.

Bring your attention inward to your thoughts. Just notice them. Be aware of each thought as it arises. Then just let it go. Continue this process of noticing and dismissing thoughts for a moment.

If you notice a particularly negative thought, notice how you feel as you pay attention to this thought. Inhale slowly and imagine that you are inflating that negative thought until it bursts and disappears. Allow the feeling to vanish with the thought.

Take a deep breath in and as you exhale bring your attention back to the flow of thoughts, allowing them to flow by like leaves in a stream.

If you notice a recurring negative thought that doesn't stop when you burst it, just notice it and deliberately change your focus to something that feels better such as the memory of a beautiful flower, a pretty face, a happy time, or a yummy food.

Take a deep breath and look around you and notice something in your surroundings that feels neutral or pleasant to look at. Perhaps the sun is shining in the window, or the wall is painted a pretty color, or you are with others who are all on a similar journey, or there is an attractive picture on the wall, or the color of the furniture is pretty, or the air smells good, or the chair is comfortable, or you can hear birds singing.

Find something neutral or positive to focus on either inside your imagination or in your surroundings.

Now take a deep breath and notice how you feel as you focus on this positive thing that exists either in your mind or in your surroundings.

How has your inner landscape changed since starting this meditation?

Continue this process for a few minutes. Notice the thought, inflate and burst it if it's negative, and if it recurs, change your focus to something that feels better either in your memory, imagination, or in your surroundings.

You can follow this process any time you notice negative thoughts.

Silence. (Modify the length of this silence depending on the needs of the client. Start small with 10 seconds and increase with practice up to 5 or 10 minutes.)

Tool 17-2: Find a Thought That Feels Better

THEORY: Depression is characterized by chronic automatic negative thoughts, which Daniel Amen calls ANTs (Amen, 1998). This tool references Tools 7-4 and 7-5, and provides a technique for clients to recognize and exterminate their ANTs by finding a thought that feels better.

IMPLEMENTATION: Explain that a hallmark of depression is chronic automatic negative thoughts. When someone is depressed, their mind gets stuck in a rut and produces a steady stream of negative and discouraging thoughts that typically are not realistic. It is as if depression places a filter over everything that only allows things through that feel bad. Use Tool 7-5 to help clients learn to recognize their ANTs and find thoughts that feel better. Encourage them to get in the habit of using this tool regularly to notice negative thoughts and quickly shift their mood.

Use the Changing the Channel Tool 7-4 as an excellent way to focus on something that feels better.

PROCESSING: Help your client reflect on the process of noticing and changing automatic negative thoughts. Did they notice automatic negative thoughts and, if so, what species were they? Were they able to find realistic thoughts that feel better? How often are they using this skill? Did they notice any changes in their depression? Have they noticed any change in their patterns of negative thinking? Is there any decrease in negative thinking? Is this getting easier with practice?

ANXIETY

Tool 17-3: Lower and Eliminate Anxiety

THEORY: Anxiety is characterized by chronic worry, restlessness, irritability, trouble concentrating, muscle tension, fatigue, and sleep disturbance. Mindfulness is an excellent modality for improving all of these symptoms. This tool discusses how to apply mindfulness tools described elsewhere in this book to anxiety.

IMPLEMENTATION: Describe the symptoms of anxiety. Explain that these symptoms are typically associated with an over-activated arousal state in the brain. Mindfulness skills routinely calm down the sympathetic nervous system which is so over-aroused in anxiety. Use any or all of the following tools to help clients with anxiety.

Mindfulness practice, calming the busy brain, and focusing on inner thoughts and feelings can sometimes (though not always) heighten anxiety in clients with an anxiety disorder or those with a low self-image. This is especially true for teens as increased self-awareness may increase the already heightened self-consciousness that often accompanies adolescence (Schonert-Reichl and Lawlor, 2010). Keep this in mind as you introduce, teach, and reflect on these various mindfulness skills for clients with anxiety.

Start small, teach breathing techniques and awareness of breath to start, and move slowly from outer focus to inner focus. Explore the client's experience as you go and adjust to ensure the client feels comfortable with the practice and knows how to handle what arises.

Mindfulness of Breath	Tools 5-1–5-7
Present Moment Awareness	Tools 6-1–6-5
Mindfulness of Thoughts	Tools 7-1–7-6

Mindfulness of Emotions	Tools 8-1–8-4
Mindfulness of Physical Body	Tools 9-1–9-5
Mindfulness of Tasks	Tools 11-1–11-3
Mindfulness of Motion	Tools 15-1–15-4

PROCESSING: Process each skill as described under the specific tool. When helping the client reflect on their experience, be on the lookout for increased anxiety. If this happens, process it with your client, teach them how to handle it, and if they can't tolerate this increased anxiety, move to more outwardly focused skills and shorten the mediation time. Then gradually increase time and move slowly to inwardly focused skills. Most clients will notice a decrease in anxiety and an increased feeling of self-control.

Tool 17-4: Change the Channel

THEORY: Anxiety can feel overwhelming to those who experience it. It often makes the person feel out of control. This tool explains how to apply the Changing the Channel tool to help clients gain a sense of control over their anxiety.

IMPLEMENTATION: Clients with anxiety often feel like their anxious thoughts take over their brain and their life. Use the Changing the Channel Tool 7-4 to help them identify something that feels calm and pleasant that they can put on their "calm" channel. Then teach them that when they notice they are feeling anxious, they can change the channel to the calm channel they previously defined. Explain that by repeatedly changing the channel to calmer thoughts they will gradually rewire their brain to be less anxious.

PROCESSING: Ask your client when they used the Changing the Channel tool. What did they put on their "calm" channel? Were they able to change the channel? What did they notice about how they felt before and after they changed the channel? Would it help to have more than one "calm" channel to choose from?

PANIC ATTACKS

Tool 17-5: Abort and Prevent Panic Attacks

THEORY: A panic attack is a discreet event that involves the sudden and intense onset of fear or discomfort and four or more of the following symptoms: (1) palpitations, pounding heart, racing heart; (2) sweating; (3) trembling or shaking; (4) shortness of breath; (5) feeling of choking; (6) chest pain; (7) nausea; (8) dizziness, lightheadedness; (9) feelings of unreality, detachment from self; (10) fear of losing control or going crazy; (11) fear of dying; (12) tingling; or (13) chills or hot flashes. Although often confused with a heart attack, a panic attack responds well to mindfulness breathing techniques that help a client calm their mind and body. This gives them a sense of control and often decreases the occurrence of further attacks. This tool teaches how to apply breathing techniques to abort and prevent panic attacks.

IMPLEMENTATION: If a client is in the midst of a panic attack, use a calm soothing voice and ask them to have a seat. Make eye contact with them. Tell them they are having a panic attack. Then tell them to take a slow, deep breath in through their nose while you count to four. Do it with them. Then ask them to exhale even more slowly, to the count of eight, and to purse their lips like they are blowing a bubble. Count to eight as you do it with them. Now lead them through another slow deep breath and an exhale to the count of eight. Ask them if they are starting to feel better. Repeat the deep breaths for up to four breaths and then stop. Ask them how they feel. Distract them by asking them about something you don't know about them: where they live, what they did today, etc. Stay totally present with them. If the breathing isn't calming them fast enough, tell them to imagine that their hands are soaking in really warm water and feel nice and warm. Tell them that their body and mind are gradually relaxing and sending warmth to their hands. Explain that as this happens they will notice their hands begin to feel heavy. Check in with them and ask how they are doing. Typically by now the panic attack has backed off. If not, start over again with the breathing and repeat.

When they are not in the midst of a panic attack, teach them the breathing techniques described in Tools 5-1 through 5-7. Encourage them to practice the breathing until they feel comfortable with it. Then if they feel a panic attack coming on, they can use the breathing techniques to head it off or at least decrease its duration and intensity. As they experience being able to prevent or calm a panic attack, they will soon discover they are having fewer of them and they may stop altogether.

PROCESSING: After the panic attack has subsided, ask the client how they feel. What, if anything, do they think triggered the attack? Has this happened before? How have they handled it before? What was different this time when they used the breathing techniques? Have they noticed a decrease in frequency or intensity of attacks as they practice the breathing techniques when not in the midst of a panic attack?

POSTTRAUMATIC STRESS DISORDER (PTSD)

Tool 17-6: Decrease PTSD Symptoms

THEORY: One characteristic of posttraumatic stress disorder (PTSD) is that the person experiences thoughts and feelings that happened during a past traumatic event as if they are happening in the present. This tool helps the client be aware of their inner thoughts and feelings, identify if they are from the past or present, and bring themselves back to the present moment.

IMPLEMENTATION: Start by teaching the Mindfulness of Breath skills from Chapter 5. Then use the Present Moment Awareness skills from Chapter 6 to help the client stay focused on the present moment instead of past experiences. Help them dismiss thoughts that are not about the present moment and bring their attention back to the present surroundings or object they have chosen to focus on. These skills will help them stay grounded in the present. Then introduce them to the Mindfulness of Thoughts and Emotions skills from Chapters 7 and 8. When you help them reflect on their experience using these skills, help them identify whether the thoughts or feelings are from the past or the present and encourage them to focus on those that are from the present.

PROCESSING: Since the thoughts and feelings that arise in PTSD often originate in the unconscious mind, use this tool to teach your client how to observe and reflect on what comes up for them instead of automatically engaging with it. This will help them make the unconscious more conscious. Help them step back and notice which thoughts and emotions are from the now and which are from the past. Then help them choose to pay attention to the components of these that are in this moment.

Tool 17-7: Havening

THEORY: Havening is a technique developed by Ronald Ruden, author of *When the Past Is Always Present* (Ruden, 2011), that has been shown to be effective in de-linking emotional experience from a trauma and thereby transforming the trauma to just an ordinary memory. Havening has three components: recall and activation of an emotional core; distraction; and havening touch. The touch provides sensory distraction to eliminate the thought and associated distress of the trauma. Touch increases the size of the delta waves in the brain, which is calming, and the distress decreases as serotonin and GABA increase. This tool provides the basic structure of the havening technique. Ruden's book provides the full explanation of the technique and the neurobiology of why it works. Visit www.Havening.org for more details.

IMPLEMENTATION: Use the process outlined in Handout 17-7 to help your client delink the traumatic event from the emotional content. Choose one component of the trauma to focus on first. While they are thinking of and feeling the distress of the trauma, distract them by asking them to sing, count, or imagine climbing stairs to their safe haven, etc., while using touch on their third eye on their forehead, their cheeks, their upper arms, and their palms. Repeat the process until the client reports a significantly reduced distress level. Then use it on other aspects of trauma your client has experienced. There is no need for them to tell you about the trauma, just for them to bring it to mind momentarily.

PROCESSING: This exercise uses counting and singing to distract the client from the trauma and to displace the traumatic thought from the working memory while touching or rubbing their forehead, cheeks, upper arms, or palms of hands. This changes the brainwave patterns, specifically the delta waves. Explain that this process provides a safe haven, which removes inescapability, which subsequently removes trauma. As you work through this process, the client usually reports feeling less and less distressed when they try to recall the traumatic event.

HANDOUT 17-7
SELF-HAVENING EXERCISE

1. Activate the emotional component of the distressing event by bringing it to mind. If a craving or compulsion is experienced, this is sufficient activation. Rate the distress level 0–10, where 0 is not at all and 10 is extreme. This is called a SUD (Subjective Units of Distress) score.

2. Begin self-havening by caressing upper arms. That is, move your hands down the upper arms. Circle outward and repeat downward stroking.

3. At the same time, with your eyes closed, visualize walking up a staircase of 20 steps. As you climb, each step causes the distress, desire, or compulsion to diminish and for you to feel safe, peaceful, and calm. Count 1–20 aloud as you climb the steps in your imagination. Continue arm self-havening.

4. After you have reached 20, begin to hum the song *Row, Row, Row Your Boat* for two rounds while continuing the arm havening. When finished, take a deep breath and open your eyes and look to the right and left. Close your eyes, inhale deeply, and slowly exhale. Continue arm havening and rate your SUD.

5. Repeat 2–4 with face havenings and palm havening (see illustrations in Handout 17-8). You may choose the same visual and song or another for variety. Other visual images can include swimming, running, jumping rope, etc. One can then hum any neutral song: *Twinkle, Twinkle Little Star; Take Me Out to the Ball Game;* or any one of your choice.

After each round (Arm, Face, Palm) rate your SUD. Continue till you reach 0 or SUD score remains stable after two additional rounds.

Used with permission from (Ruden, 2013).

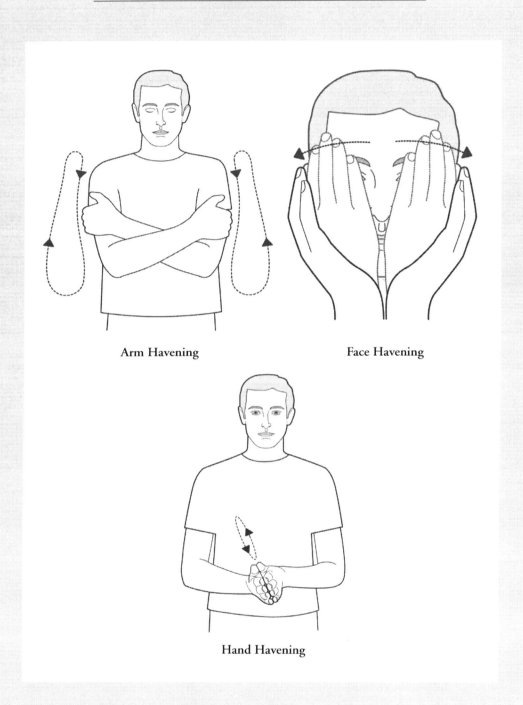

Arm Havening

Face Havening

Hand Havening

Used with permission of Ronald Ruden.

OBSESSIVE COMPULSIVE DISORDER

Tool 17-8: Increase Awareness of Obsessional Thinking

THEORY: Dan Siegel (Siegel, 2010) explains one way to think about obsessive thoughts is to realize they are typically trying to keep us safe. He names the source of these thoughts "the checker," which is always checking to make sure we are safe and that we survive. He discusses how this checker often goes overboard to alert us to danger. This tool helps the client to re-frame their obsessional thinking and to begin to be able to recognize their "checker" at work.

IMPLEMENTATION: Explain that each time your client has an obsessional thought, they can simply notice that their "checker" is trying to help them out, or keep them safe—even when this help is not rational, effective, or needed. Use Awareness of Breath (Tools 5-1 through 5-7), Thoughts (Tools 7-1 through 7-6), and Emotions (Tools 8-1 through 8-4) to help your client gradually learn to identify and observe the obsessional thinking without engaging in it or responding with compulsive actions. Help your client to notice the checker at work and then to begin to understand when their checker is helpful and when it is overreacting.

PROCESSING: Ask your client what they notice about their obsessional thinking as they do the mindfulness exercises. Explore when they have been able to identify their checker at work. Discuss how they can tell when the checker is being helpful and when the checker is overreacting. How has their obsessional thinking changed through the process of mindfulness practice? Have their obsessional thoughts decreased in intensity?

Tool 17-9: Decrease Obsessional Thinking and Compulsions

THEORY: Dan Siegel describes a process for talking back to the internal checker and thereby reducing obsessional thinking, which he playfully calls "thanks for sharing" (Siegel, 2010). It involves identifying recurrent thoughts that are typically irrational and simply don't go away as being generated by their checker in an effort to keep them safe—see Tool 17-8. This tool provides the next step to talk to the checker in a way that acknowledges its efforts to keep you safe, thank it for its help, and then tell it you don't need quite that much help right now.

IMPLEMENTATION: Explain that the checker is trying to keep your client safe, but typically goes way overboard with concern. Now that your client is getting better at recognizing their checker at work (see Tool 17-8), help them establish an inner dialogue with their checker that acknowledges the checker's effort to keep them safe, thanks it, soothes it, and lets it know they are safe. An example might be if a client has an obsession based on irrational fear of going to the grocery store (which may be one of many such obsessions). When they think about going to a grocery store, their checker might say, "Uh, oh! Don't go in that store. Someone might make fun of you." The client might respond inside their head with, "Thanks for sharing, checker. Thanks for your protection and love. I know you want to keep me safe. I want to be safe. But you are being too protective now, and it's not necessary to keep me safe. The grocery store is a safe place for me." Encourage your client to keep an inner dialogue with their checker to keep their checker "in check," so to speak.

PROCESSING: Help your client reflect on when they noticed that their checker was overreacting. Review how they talked with their checker and how it changed their obsessional thinking. Explore how it feels to address their obsessions in this manner.

BIPOLAR DISORDER

Tool 17-10: Awareness of Mood State

THEORY: Bipolar disorder is characterized by wide mood swings that range from major depression to mania. Mindfulness skills have been shown to improve depression, decrease anxiety, and generally improve brain regulation and mood stabilization. This tool explains how to use mindfulness skills to increase awareness of mood state for clients with bipolar disorder.

IMPLEMENTATION: Explain to your client that the first step in decreasing their mood swings is to be able to be aware of their current mood state so they will recognize when it begins to swing. Help them learn to do this by teaching them Awareness of Breath, Thoughts, and Emotions mindfulness skills (Tools in Chapters 5, 7, and 8). Using these skills, they will gradually improve their ability to be aware of their inner emotional landscape at any given moment as well as thoughts associated with different moods.

PROCESSING: Help your client reflect on their experience with these mindfulness skills. What feelings and mood state have they been able to identify? What thoughts precede any particular emotion? Are they able to notice emotions as they arise? Are they gaining awareness of when their mood state begins to swing?

Tool 17-11: Stabilize Mood

THEORY: Once someone with bipolar disorder has increased awareness of their inner emotional landscape at any given moment (Tool 17-10), then they can use specific mindfulness skills to increase brain regulation and thereby stabilize mood swings. This tool provides resources for mindfulness skills that will aid in stabilizing the brain.

IMPLEMENTATION: After your client has increased their ability to be aware of their internal emotional landscape (Tool 17-10), the next step is to encourage them to use various guided meditations such as Progressive Relaxation (Tool 9-3), Remembered Wellness (Tool 9-4), and Core Heart Feelings (Tool 8-3) as well as Mindfulness of Tasks (Tools 11-1 and 11-2). As they practice, and their skill increases, encourage them to practice a more formal core sitting meditation (Tool 5-4), starting with a brief period and gradually increasing to longer meditation time. Typically, as their ability to sit in this type of practice increases, their brain will become more regulated. The more they practice this while not in a manic state, the less frequent and intense their manic episodes may become.

Case Example

A man was hospitalized during a manic episode. He had been hospitalized numerous times before, but this was his first hospitalization in quite some time. He stated that since his last hospitalization, he had started meditating on a regular basis. He noticed that his moods were more stable, and his highs less high, and lows less low. His meditation practice allowed him to hold a part-time job for the first time since going on disability due to his bipolar disorder. This episode of mania was much shorter than previous episodes that had resulted in hospitalization and responded quickly to a small change in medication.

PROCESSING: Help your client reflect on their experience with the various meditation practices as described in each tool. Help them track their moods and become aware of how their cycles may be changing in duration and intensity.

Chapter 18: ADHD

Tool 18-1: Increase Concentration
Tool 18-2: Reduce Hyperactivity

Tool 18-1: Increase Concentration

THEORY: One study showed that mindfulness practice improves concentration and reduces hyperactivity for teens and adults with ADHD (Zylowska et al, 2008). There is also much anecdotal clinical evidence that it helps children with ADHD as well. Other studies show improved concentration in people without ADHD.

This tool refers to the many mindfulness skills that may be helpful to someone with ADHD. It then describes a technique that helps children and adults use their imagination to pretend they are doing an activity while continually bringing their attention back to the task at hand. This practice, when done repeatedly, gradually improves their ability to stay focused when they are doing that (or another) task.

IMPLEMENTATION: Most of the tools in this workbook can be used to improve concentration. Introduce your clients to the various tools in this workbook starting with basic breathing techniques, mindfulness of breath, mindfulness of tasks, and walking meditations. Remember to start with brief periods of sitting still and introspection for people with ADHD and slowly increase length of meditations as skill improves. People with ADHD may be put off by longer periods, so start small and work up.

The two brief mindfulness exercises provided in Handouts 18-1A and 18-1B can be used for adults or students of any age depending on their situation. Read either of the meditations to your client and ask them to reflect on what came up for them during the exercise. It will increase the effectiveness of this exercise if you can repeat it a number of times over the course of a few weeks. Recommend that they remember the exercise when they are actually getting ready in the morning or sitting in the classroom to remind themselves to notice when they are distracted and to bring their attention back to what they need to be paying attention to.

PROCESSING: Ask the client to reflect on what happened for them during the exercise. Were they able to use their imagination to visualize as you were guiding them? How did they stay focused during the exercise? At a subsequent session, ask them if they were able to remind themselves to stay focused as in the exercise. How did saying "not now" or "maybe later" help them?

HANDOUT 18-1A
INCREASE CONCENTRATION

In the Classroom

Close your eyes and listen to my voice. Pretend you are in school. Imagine you are sitting in your chair at your desk. Can you feel the chair on your bottom and against your back? What does the desk feel like when you touch it with your hands? Does the desk top lift up? What do you keep in your desk? Look inside. Can you see what's in your desk? Do you have everything you need?

Imagine what the classroom smells like. Does it smell familiar? Look at who is sitting next to you. Are you friends? Do you get along?

Where is the teacher? Is the teacher talking to the class? Listen to the teacher. What does the teacher want you to learn? Is the classroom noisy or quiet? If the student next to you tries to talk to you while the teacher is talking, tell them, "not now" and look back at the teacher's eyes and lips. Pay close attention to what the teacher is saying. If there is noise in the hall or outside the window, just notice it but then pretend you are looking right at the teacher's lips and eyes again. What does the teacher want you to do?

Practice paying attention to the teacher and to your work every time you are in class.

Handout 18-1B
Increase Concentration

Getting Ready on Time

Close your eyes and use your imagination to pretend that it is morning and you are still in bed. Listen to my voice as I describe your morning routine. Imagine that the alarm clock just buzzed and you hit the button to turn it off. Take a deep breath and let it out slowly. Open your eyes and look around the bedroom to wake yourself up. Think about your plans for the day and what time you need to be ready to leave the house. If you tend to fall back to sleep, think about what happens when you are late and how much better you feel when you are on time. Get up and start your morning routine.

Go to the bathroom and then brush your teeth. If you are distracted and want to do something like watch TV, tell yourself, "Another time; I'm getting ready on time now" and bring your attention back to brushing your teeth. As you take a shower, stay focused on getting clean, washing your hair, rinsing, and perhaps shaving. As you notice that you are thinking about something besides taking a shower, gently bring your attention back to the shower and what you are doing. Focus on washing each part of your body, turn off the water, grab a towel, and dry off.

As you fix your hair and perhaps do your makeup, pay attention to each task. When you notice your mind has wandered, just notice it and bring your attention back to what you are doing. If you are tempted to do something besides fixing your hair or doing your makeup, remind yourself what you are doing, say "Maybe later," and bring you attention back on task.

While you are picking out something to wear, stay focused on finding an outfit to wear today. If you discover you are off task and doing something else instead, gently say "Not now" and get back to choosing your outfit. As you get dressed, keep your attention on getting dressed. If someone comes in the room and distracts you, tell them, "Not now; I'm getting dressed."

How are you doing? Go to the kitchen and get something to eat. Doesn't it feel good when you have stayed on task so well that you have plenty of time for breakfast? As you eat, keep your mind on the smell, taste, and texture of the food. When your mind wanders, just bring it back to focus on eating. If someone asks you to do something for them, tell them, "Not now; I'm eating."

When you are done eating, spend a few minutes helping out anyone who asked you to help them. Be mindful of the time.

When it is 5 minutes before you need to leave, gather everything you need for the day (hopefully, you got it ready last night), and leave the house. Notice how good it feels to be on time.

Now that you have used your imagination to stay focused and be ready on time, practice this process every morning until it becomes automatic.

Tool 18-2: Reduce Hyperactivity

THEORY: People with the hyperactive/impulsive type or the combined type of ADHD often have difficulty sitting still. Children may get out of their seat, run around, climb, jump up and down, and otherwise constantly move. Adults may fidget, tap their fingers or feet, swing their foot, or perhaps just experience a feeling of restlessness. This tool describes a fun game called "Balancing Chips" that can be played with clients to help them become more aware of their body and its constant motion. Often, with practice, this awareness increases, they gain more control over their body motion, and become more able to stay still.

IMPLEMENTATION: Explain to your client that you are going to play a Balancing Chips game with them to see how long they can stay still. Follow the guidelines provided in Handout 18-2. Make it fun and challenge them to see how long they can keep the chips from falling off. Do it over and over and observe if they can balance them longer and longer with practice.

PROCESSING: Discuss what you observed about their ability to lie still. Ask them what it felt like to keep the chips from falling off. Did they have trouble lying still? Were they able to lie still? If so, how did they keep still? Did they have fun? Were they able to stay still longer as they practiced? How did it feel to stay still? Ask them to notice when they are having trouble staying still and to remember how it felt to lie completely still.

HANDOUT 18-2
BALANCING CHIPS GAME

Use the chips from a game such as Checkers, Othello, or Connect Four. Take them out and place them where you and the client can reach them. We are going to play a Mindful Body game called Balancing Chips. Please lie down on the floor on your back with your arms and legs straight. Now I will give you a chip. Take the chip and place it on your leg just above your ankle and balance it there. Now put this next chip on the other leg. Now put this next chip on your leg above your knee and this next chip on the other leg. If it is okay with you, I will put the rest of the chips on. I will put one chip on the back of each hand and then another chip on each arm between your wrist and your elbow. I will put a chip on each shoulder. Now I will put a chip on each side of your forehead above your eyes. And I will put this last chip on your chin.

"Now I will time how long you can balance all of these chips without moving and knocking any of them off. Pay attention to your breathing. Allow yourself to relax and sink into the floor. If you feel you need to move, just let go of that thought and bring your attention back to how it feels to breathe."

Keep track of how long they balance the chips before they move and start knocking the chips off. Make it fun. Let them try several times. Time them and see if they can stay still longer. Then let them play the game a few weeks later after learning and practicing more mindfulness skills. They may start to decrease hyperactivity and gain more control over their body movement as their awareness of their body increases.

Chapter 19: Medical Illness, Pain, and Sleep Disorders

CHRONIC PAIN
>Tool 19-1: Pain Management

CHRONIC MEDICAL ILLNESS
>Tool 19-2: Remembered Wellness

SLEEP DISORDERS
>Tool 19-3: Meditation for Sleep

CHRONIC PAIN

Tool 19-1: Pain Management

THEORY: Mindfulness meditation has been shown to be helpful with chronic pain (Kabat-Zinn et al., 1986). There is a natural tendency to tighten or clench around the painful area, which tends to increase pain. It is also common to want to escape or distract oneself from pain or ignore it until it becomes unbearable. If only we had paid attention to that little voice inside when it said, "I'm uncomfortable. Please rest or take a short break." This tool provides several options for increasing awareness of pain, accepting and if possible releasing body tension, staying present, and dealing with the underlying thoughts and emotions that accompany pain.

IMPLEMENTATION: The first step in managing pain with mindfulness is to increase awareness of body pain and tension while accepting it or, at a minimum, letting it be. This can be done by using the Body Scan Tool 9-1, which guides the client to check in with each area of the body, notice what's there, acknowledge it, and if possible release any tension or discomfort. The Progressive Relaxation Tool 9-3 can be used to release and relax muscle tension, which will assist in reducing pain. The Remembered Wellness Tool 9-4 can be used to help your client remember a time when they were pain-free and imagine feeling better. Guide your client to check in with their body at regular intervals, perhaps even setting an alarm to remind them to do so. Ask them to ask themselves, "How is my body?" and to notice what's there without resistance or judgment. Teach them to tune in to their pain as an observer and to resist tightening up the muscles around the pain. Encourage them to take short breaks on a regular basis.

The second step in managing pain with mindfulness is to help your client deal with the uncomfortable emotions that often accompany physical pain. Use the Mindfulness of Emotions Tools 8-1 through 8-4 to help them observe and be aware of emotions, without engaging with them, and to help them allow the ebb and flow of emotions that will occur with pain without judging the experience. Use the Mindfulness of Thoughts Tools 7-1 through 7-6 to help them allow thoughts to come and go without engaging and to find thoughts that feel better.

The third step in dealing with pain is increasing the ability to live in the present moment. Use a variety of the mindfulness tools included in this workbook including the Present Moment Awareness Tools 6-1 through 6-7 to help your client practice staying in the here and now.

PROCESSING: Explore with your client how they typically deal with their pain. Do they try to ignore it? Does it overwhelm them and take all their attention? Does it interfere with their functioning? Ask your client to reflect on what they notice about their pain when they do a body scan. Do they find body tension around the pain? Are they able to release the tension even a little bit? Are they afraid that if they pay attention to their pain it will get worse? How does the Progressive Relaxation exercise change their pain? Are they getting better at checking in with their body and perhaps taking a short rest when they need to? If so, how does this change their pain? What is their story behind the pain? Explore what their expectations are about the future of the pain. What emotions accompany their pain? What is their relationship to their pain? How does staying present in the moment change their experience?

CHRONIC MEDICAL ILLNESS

Tool 19-2: Remembered Wellness

THEORY: Studies show that mindfulness practices can improve many types of physical illness (Tool 2-20). Herbert Benson teaches the concept of remembered wellness (Benson, 1996). Remembered wellness is based on the idea that our brains don't know the difference between actually feeling well or remembering a time when we felt well. Therefore, by remembering a time we felt well, we help our brain recreate the internal conditions that were present at that time. This tool provides a Remembered Wellness meditation designed to tap into the power of healing by remembering a time when the client felt well and imaging that they feel well in the present moment.

IMPLEMENTATION: Explain the concept of remembered wellness to your client. Tell them that by remembering a time that they felt well, they set up the conditions in their brain to recreate that wellness in the present. Read the Remembered Wellness meditation that's included on Handout 9-4 to them. Afterwards, ask them if they were able to find a time that they felt well. Encourage them to repeat this meditation on a regular basis. Be aware that this meditation can initially provoke sadness and feelings of loss for some people as they remember how good they used to feel as they get in touch with losses they may have incurred due to poor health.

PROCESSING: Ask your client if they were able to remember a time that they felt well. Explore their memory of feeling well. Were they able to remember how it felt when they felt well? What did they notice about how they felt in the present as they did the meditation? Did they notice any change in their body or their emotions? Did they experience a sense of loss or sadness? If so, process these feelings, validate them, and normalize them. Give them a realistic sense of how practicing remembered wellness works to shift them into a healthier state.

SLEEP DISORDERS

Tool 19-3: Meditation for Sleep

THEORY: In the 1970s Harvard cardiologist Herbert Benson coined the term "relaxation response" as described in his book of the same name (Benson, 2000). The relaxation response elicits a state of deep relaxation in which our breathing, pulse rate, blood pressure, and metabolism are decreased. This tool provides a Meditation for Sleep that provides a progressive relaxation combined with guided imagery designed to invoke the relaxation response to improve the listener's ability to relax and fall asleep.

IMPLEMENTATION: Explain the basics of the relaxation response to your client, including how doing a relaxing mindfulness meditation can counter the effects of the fight, flight, or freeze stress response. Handout 19-3 contains the text of a Meditation for Sleep. You or your client can read it aloud and record it so it can be listened to at night when going to sleep. Explain that they will gradually notice their mind and body relaxing as they listen. They will be more able to turn off the busy chatter of their brain and enter into a drowsy state conducive to falling asleep. Encourage your client to listen to the Meditation for Sleep in bed every night at bedtime. Have them make sure that whatever they use to play the recording will turn off by itself and not need their attention, which would interfere with sleep.

PROCESSING: After assigning this exercise, ask your client if they have been using the Meditation for Sleep. If not, explore why not and brainstorm with them about how to incorporate it into their bedtime routine. If they have used it, explore what they experienced. Did it help them relax? Did it help them fall asleep? What did they notice about their sleep and their ability to stay asleep when they used it? What did they notice about their body tension, comfort, discomfort? Did they experience any emotions as they listened? Were they distracted and, if so, by what? How did they bring their attention back to the meditation? What might they need to change in their bedroom to encourage sleep, such as removing the TV, computer, and other distractions, making sure the bed is comfortable, the room is dark and quiet, and that they get to bed at the same time every night?

Let's begin by doing a few deep cleansing breaths. Breathe in through your nose to the count of four and breathe out through your mouth to the count of eight. Purse your lips as you blow out, like gently blowing a bubble.

Do it with me. Breathe in through your nose and then, as you exhale, relax your mind. Do it again. Breathe in relaxation and, as you breathe out, relax your mind. One more time. Breathe in comfort and, as you breathe out, let go of anything that needs to go.

Now breathe normally.

Pay attention to your toes. Notice how they feel. Notice if there is any tightness or discomfort there and let it flow right out through the ends of your toes and onto the floor.

Now focus on your feet: the balls of your feet, your arches, your heels, the tops of your feet. Just pay attention to what's there and let anything that needs to go flow right out through the ends of your toes and onto the floor.

Now concentrate on your ankles. Just notice what they feel like. Send them loving thoughts. Allow any discomfort or tension stored there to flow down through your feet and right through the ends of your toes and onto the floor.

Now bring your awareness to your calves and shins. Again, just notice what's there. Let anything that needs to go flow right down through your ankles, your feet, and right through the ends of your toes and onto the floor.

Now bring your attention to your knees. Notice what they feel like. Let go of anything that doesn't belong. Let it flow down through your calves and shins, through your ankles, your feet, and right through the ends of your toes and onto the floor.

Now bring your awareness to your thighs. Notice what's there and allow anything that needs to go to flow down through your knees, your calves and shins, your feet, and right through the ends of your toes and onto the floor.

Now focus on your bottom. Pay attention to what you notice there. Just let go of anything that needs to go and let it flow down through your thighs, through your knees, your calves and shins, your feet, and right through the ends of your toes and onto the floor.

Now bring your attention to your lower belly or abdomen. Spend a moment to notice what you are carrying there. Allow anything that doesn't belong to flow down through your thighs, through your knees, your calves and shins, your feet, and right through the ends of your toes and onto the floor.

Now notice how your lower back feels. Lots of tension gets stored here and you just don't need any of it. Let it flow down through your bottom, your thighs, through your knees, your calves and shins, your feet, and right through the ends of your toes and onto the floor.

Now concentrate on your stomach. Imagine that you are looking at a rope that is twisted, coiled, and tied up tightly. But as you watch the rope it unwinds, uncoils, and unties until it is hanging limply. Image that your stomach and the area around your stomach have done the same and are now relaxed and comfortable.

Bring your awareness to your chest and heart area. Take a nice deep breath in through your nose and fill your lungs with a cushion of healing energy. As you breathe out, allow everything that needs to go to flow out.

Now pay attention to your middle and upper back. Lots of stuff gets carried here and you don't need any of it. Allow it to flow down through your lower back, your bottom, through your thighs, through your knees, your calves and shins, your feet, and right through the ends of your toes and onto the floor.

Now focus on your neck and shoulders. Again, lots of tightness gets stored here and you don't need it. Allow it to flow down your back, through your bottom, through your thighs, through your knees, your calves and shins, your feet, and right through the ends of your toes and onto the floor.

Now pay attention to your hands including your fingers, thumbs, palms, and backs of your hands. Notice what you carry here and let go of anything you don't need. Let it flow through the ends of your fingers and onto the floor.

Now pay attention to your arms including your forearms, elbows, upper arms right on up to your shoulders. Let anything you don't need flow down through your arms, your wrists, your hands, and right through the ends of your fingers and onto the floor.

Now raise your awareness to your face including your jaw, cheeks, eyes, and forehead. Drop your jaw and just let it hang totally limp. Let any tension stored in your face flow down through your neck, shoulders, arms, hands, and right through the ends of your fingers and onto the floor.

Now pay attention to your brain. As thoughts arise, imagine they are written on a blank white board. As soon as you see them there, erase them and imagine the board empty again.

Now that your body is completely relaxed and starting to doze, imagine that you are walking along a path in the forest. Take a slow deep breath. The air smells so good here, so clean and natural. You feel connected to the earth. You can hear the birds singing. You notice how the sun is shining down through the leaves and creating beautiful patterns of sunlight and shadow on the forest floor. The forest floor is lush and green. You feel so happy, alive, and content.

As you walk along, you gradually reach the edge of the forest and walk into a beautiful meadow. The air is clear, the sun is shining, the sky is blue, and the temperature is just perfect. You can see pretty butterflies and beautiful flowers all around you. You notice the path here is worn smooth from many feet so you sit down and take off your shoes and socks. You walk along the path barefoot and you feel the smooth, warm earth on the bottoms of your feet. You feel connected to the earth and nature and infinite intelligence.

The path starts to get sandy, and you realize you are walking toward a beautiful lake. You can smell the freshness of the water and the wet sand. The water on the lake is so calm it looks like a mirror. You can see the trees perfectly reflected in the lake about the edges. The sky is blue and the air feels fresh and clean. You can see some flowers blooming at the edge of the beach and some lilies growing off the shore. Listen carefully. You can hear the water as it gently laps up against the shore. Mmm . . . it feels good here, so peaceful, so safe. If you feel like it, walk along the edge of the water and feel the cool, clear water on your feet.

As you walk, you look ahead on the beach and see a chaise lounge sitting on the sand. You walk over to it and lie down on it. It has soft cushions and it feels so comfortable when you lie down. You notice a blanket under the chaise and you reach down to get the blanket and cover yourself with it. You snuggle down.

As you lie on the chaise, you let your mind slow down some more. You let go and any busy thoughts disappear as you tell your monkey brain to calm down and relax. You feel warm and cozy. As you take some slow deep breaths, you begin to feel warm and heavy all over your body. Your eyelids get so heavy you can't keep them open anymore. Allow them to close. Listen to my voice as you let go of your day and begin to drift and allow sleep to come to you.

You realize you are in your own comfortable bed. You are safe. You feel so comfortable and relaxed. You fall into a deep restful sleep. You sleep soundly all night. You will awake in the morning exactly when you need to be awake to start your day and you will feel completely rested, rejuvenated, and wide awake. You will have the right amount of energy and you feel happy. You look forward to your day. You will notice you are completely focused and you can concentrate effortlessly. You will know what you need to do and you will get everything done that you need to do. You will be on time. You will get along with everyone and your friends and family will be happy to see you. You will stay focused, calm, relaxed, and happy all day. You know you will sleep well again at night.

Sleeping is easy now. Allow your brain to let go. Allow sleep to arrive. Sleep is here now. Sleep, sleep, sleep. Goodnight.

Chapter 20: Stress, Anger

STRESS
    Tool 20-1: Reduce Stress Response

ANGER
    Tool 20-2: Calm That Anger

STRESS

Tool 20-1: Reduce Stress Response

THEORY: The stress response is the physiological reaction to anything that is perceived as stressful, dangerous, or threatening. This is often called the flight, fight, or freeze response. This can include increased heart rate, blood pressure, stress hormones such as cortisol, and anything that makes a person fast and strong in order to survive danger. This helped our ancestors survive when they were confronted with a wild animal and they needed to run away to escape or fight to the death. In today's society people are often chronically stressed and their stress response remains too high much of the time. This may result in the onset of a variety of stress-related illness. A variety of types of mindfulness exercises effectively lowers the stress response. This tool provides guidance on how to use mindfulness tools to lower the stress response.

IMPLEMENTATION: Explain what the stress response is. Compare it to the relaxation response, which counters the stress response. Many of the mindfulness exercises in this workbook will help to lower the stress response. Teach the Basic Relaxation Breathing technique (Tool 5-1), which works to calm down the physiology by activating the parasympathetic nervous system. Then use the Mindfulness of Physical Body (Tools 9-1 through 9-5) to help reduce body tension and induce relaxation. Show them how to take their pulse to help them monitor how their heart rate responds to stress. Encourage them to use a deep relaxation breath to calm the stress response anytime they notice they feel stressed. Urge them to incorporate a variety of mindfulness exercises on a regular basis that calm their stress response.

PROCESSING: Ask your client to notice how their body feels. As they practice the various mindfulness exercises, help them reflect on what they notice in their body as well as in their mind. Explore what changes they notice in how stressed they feel as they practice mindfulness. Encourage them to remember how they feel at the end of a mindfulness exercise and then when they feel stressed, to take a few deep cleansing breaths while remembering that feeling.

ANGER

Tool 20-2: Calm That Anger

THEORY: Anger is typically a response to feeling threatened in some way. When a person feels angry, their physiology is activated much as it is in a stress response. Therefore, the mindfulness skills that work for stress will work for anger as well. This tool provides guidance on how to use mindfulness to help manage and decrease anger.

IMPLEMENTATION: A key to success in managing anger is the ability to stop for a moment before reacting to whatever triggered the anger. Use the stoplight graphic in Handout 20-2 to explain the process of stopping (red light) when the angry feeling is first noticed, thinking about possible responses (yellow light), and then choosing a wise response (green light). Then teach the basic relaxation breath and encourage your client to use this as soon as they notice they feel angry to stop (red light) to allow them to calm down (yellow light) and make a wise choice (green light). Urge them to practice the Mindfulness of Physical Body (Tools 9-1 through 9-5) and of Mindfulness of Emotion exercises (Tools 8-1 through 8-4) to help them keep their overall stress level lower and thereby help them gain control over their anger.

PROCESSING: Ask your client if they had any times when they felt angry during the week to help them begin to increase their awareness of their anger. Explore what triggered the angry feeling. Help them determine if the angry feeling was from the present or rather the past. Explore whether the anger is a chronic feeling. Explore options for addressing and reducing the triggers. Discuss what they can do to let go of the anger or transform it into a more positive feeling. Ask them to reflect on how using the "stop, think, choose" process described here with the stoplight graphic changed their anger or their angry reaction.

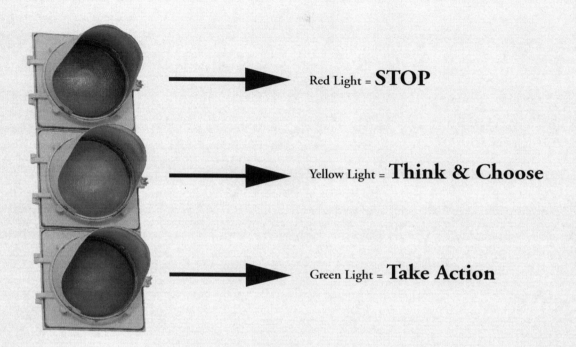

Red Light = STOP

Yellow Light = **Think & Choose**

Green Light = **Take Action**

Chapter 21: Chronic Mental Illness

SCHIZOPHRENIA
> Tool 21-1: Awareness of Surroundings and Thoughts for Grounding
> Tool 21-2: Choose Rational Thoughts

SCHIZOPHRENIA

Tool 21-1: Awareness of Surroundings and Thoughts for Grounding

THEORY: One hallmark of schizophrenia is auditory hallucinations wherein the person hears voices. Typically these voices say nasty, negative things to the person about himself and/or others. Often the schizophrenic client hears a nearly continuous running dialogue. Some clients with schizophrenia report that these voices are evil spirits that reside outside of them. They often struggle to stay present as their attention is drawn inward to their voices. This mindfulness tool provides a way for the client to shift their attention from the voices to their immediate surroundings. This can help them to be better grounded and to stay more present instead of focusing on their inner dialogue.

IMPLEMENTATION: Explain that this mindfulness exercise will help them relax and stay focused on the present moment instead of being totally distracted by their voices. Begin by teaching them Basic Relaxation Breathing (Tool 5-1). Then teach them the Present Moment Awareness Tools starting with the Mindfulness of Surroundings Tool (6-1), and then the Awareness of Object (Tools 6-3 and 6-4). Encourage them to practice this skill several times throughout their day when they hear voices and a few times when they don't hear voices.

PROCESSING: Help your client reflect on what happened for them when they practiced this skill. Did they feel more relaxed after doing the breathing exercise? Were they able to focus on their surroundings or the object during the Present Moment Awareness exercises? Did their voices distract them? How did they bring their attention back to the present moment? Do they feel like they are gaining a sense of control over what they pay attention to? Do the voices subside or get louder when they focus on the present moment?

Tool 21-2: Choose Rational Thoughts

THEORY: The voices heard by the schizophrenic client usually consist of a flow of chronically negative statements. This tool helps them find rational, realistic thoughts that feel better than the negative thoughts their voices want them to believe.

IMPLEMENTATION: Explain that this mindfulness exercise is designed to help them deal with the steady stream of negative statements their voices tell them. Use some of the Mindfulness of Thoughts (Tools 7-1 through 7-6) exercises to help them notice a thought and learn to dismiss it without engaging in it. This will help them avoid engaging with the negative statements the voices say. Then teach them to use Automatic Negative Thoughts (Tool 7-5) exercises to replace the negative thoughts that are constantly generated by the statements of their voices, with realistic thoughts that feel better. For example, if a client hears their neighbor's voice saying they think the client is stupid (when it is not possible for them to actually be hearing the neighbor), help them be aware of this thought and replace it with a more positive thought such as, "Even though I hear my neighbor saying nasty things about me, I know I am a good person and people really appreciate the yard work I do." Help the client find positive realistic thoughts that apply to their life. Encourage them to use this technique at least for short periods at a time and to notice how they feel.

PROCESSING: Discuss what the content of their voices' statements tend to be. Ask them if they were able to notice the thoughts associated with the statements. Were they able to find a thought that feels better? Help them with specific examples to counter negative statements made by their voices. Were they able to believe the thoughts they replaced the negative thoughts with? How did they feel when they did this exercise? How did their voices react when they did this exercise?

Section V

TOOLS FOR TRACKING PROGRESS

Chapter 22: Tracking Progress

Tool 22-1: Define Treatment Goals

THEORY: Defining treatment goals is important for several reasons. First, by defining treatment goals the client is setting an intention to focus on meeting these goals. Second, the treatment goals clarify and provide structure for the work to be done with the client. Third, best practice methods and most managed-care insurance companies require them. This tool discusses the process of defining treatment goals related to mindfulness practice.

IMPLEMENTATION: Ask the client how they will know if working with you has helped them. This directly addresses what their treatment goals are. Ask them for 5 to 10 goals that they would like to achieve or symptoms they would like to improve. Refer to Handout 22-1 for examples of treatment goals that research indicates may be improved with mindfulness practice.

PROCESSING: Assist the client in mindfully defining their treatment goals. Ask them to reflect on what the process was like for them. How was it helpful to clarify what they hope to improve/achieve? Encourage them to update these goals periodically.

HANDOUT 22-1
SAMPLE TREATMENT GOALS

Studies show that the following symptoms have improved with mindfulness practice. See Tool 2-22.

Client will learn and practice Mindfulness skills to:

- Improve concentration
- Manage chronic pain
- Increase emotion regulation
- Improve mood
- Decrease anxiety
- Stabilize mood swings
- Improve sleep
- Increase sense of well-being
- Improve relationships
- Improve health
- Improve stress management skills
- Reduce hyperactivity
- Decrease anger
- Improve memory
- Increase task completion
- Identify and explore feelings
- Decrease rumination
- Improve self-awareness
- Increase ability to repair negative mood states
- Decrease binge eating
- Improve self-esteem
- Improve compassion for self and others
- Improve ability to deal with chronic illness
- Quit smoking
- Reduce alcohol use

Tool 22-2: Symptom Tracking

THEORY: Tracking client progress is helpful for several reasons. First, it keeps the treatment focused on meeting treatment goals. Second, it provides a way for therapist and client to track improvement and monitor symptoms/goals as work progresses. Third, it provides a way to assess the effectiveness of treatment. This tool describes one technique for tracking symptoms or monitoring treatment goals.

IMPLEMENTATION: After defining treatment goals using Tool 22-1, ask clients to rate each symptom/goal on a scale of zero to 10 where 10 is worst and zero is no problem. List the goals/symptoms in the left-hand column of Handout 22-2B. Then place the date at the top of the next column and fill in their rating of each goal/symptom. Tally the total at the bottom. The goal will be to lower the rating on each symptom and the overall total as treatment progresses. Ask clients to rate their symptoms/goals periodically as treatment progress. Show them how their ratings are improving. See Handout 22-2A for an example of a partially completed symptom rating form.

A few clients may have trouble rating a symptom with a number. They may find it easier to describe changes they are noticing. That's okay. If possible, use this information to rate the symptoms yourself. Or, skip the numeric rating and keep a log of changes they report.

PROCESSING: Some clients find this process easy while a few do not. The goal of this tool is to provide a way to notice change and document symptom improvement. Encourage clients to rate symptoms. Most will provide a consistently accurate rating over time. Showing them their progress inspires hope and motivation for continuing their mindful practice.

HANDOUT 22-2A
CLIENT SYMPTOM/GOAL RATING CHART

SYMPTOM	11/7/11	11/14/11	11/21/11	12/2/12	DATE																					
Concentration	10	9.5	9	8																						
Depression	8	8	7.5	7																						
Anxiety	5	4	4	3																						
Sleep	6	5	4	4																						
Stress Mgt	8	7	6	5																						
TOTAL Score	37	33.50	30.5	27																						

DATE																							

SYMPTOM

TOTAL Score

APPENDIX
References

Alidina, S. (2011). *Mindfulness for dummies.* West Sussex, England: John Wiley & Sons, Ltd.

Ame, Daniel. (1998) *Change your brain change your life.* New York, NY: Random House, 1998.

Baba, Sri Siva. "The Light Connection." *Life Connecting Magazine.* Retrieved November 8, 2012, from www.lightconnection.us/Archive/jun09/jun09_article2.html.

Baer, R. A., Smith, G. T., Lykins, E., Button, D., Krietemeyer, J., Sauer, S., Walsh, E., Duggan, D., and Williams, J. M. Construct validity of the five facet mindfulness questionnaire in meditating and nonmeditating samples. *Assessment.* 2008; 15: 329–342.

Baer, R. A. Mindfulness training as clinical intervention: A conceptual and empirical review. *Clinical Psychology: Science and Practice.* 2003; 10: 125–143.

Baer, R. A., Smith, G. T., Hopkins, J., Krietemeyer, J., and Toney, L. Using self-report assessment methods to explore facets of mindfulness. *Assessment.* 2006; 13: 27–45.

Benson, H. (2000). *The relaxation response.* (Updated). New York, NY: William Morrow Paperbacks.

Benson, H., and Friedman, R. Harnessing the power of the placebo effect and renaming it "remembered wellness." *Annual Review of Medicine.* 1996; 47: 193-199.

Bowen, S., Witkiewitz, K., Dillworth, T. M., et al. Mindfulness meditation and substance use in an incarcerated population. *Psychology of Addictive Behaviors.* 2006; 20: 343–347.

Brown, K. W., Ryan, R. M., and Creswell, J. D. Mindfulness: Theoretical foundations and evidence for salutary effects. *Psychological Inquiry.* 2007; 18: 211–237.

Brown, K. W., and Ryan, R. M. The benefits of being present: Mindfulness and its role in psychological well-being. *Journal of Personality and Social Psychology.* 2003; 84: 822–848.

Burke C. Mindfulness-Based Approaches with Children and Adolescents: A Preliminary Review of Current Research in an Emergent Field. *J Child Fam Stud. 2009.* Retrieved November 8, 2012, from www.mindfulschools.org/pdf/burke-child-adol.pdf.

Cahn, B. R., and Polich, J. Meditation states and traits: EEG, ERP, and neuroimaging studies. *Psychological Bulletin.* 2006; 132: 180–211.

Cardaciotto, L., Herbert, J. D., et al. The assessment of present-moment awareness and acceptance: The Philadelphia mindfulness scale. *Assessment.* 2008; 15: 204–223.

Carmody, J., and Baer, R. A. Relationships between mindfulness practice and levels of mindfulness, medical and psychological symptoms and well-being in a mindfulness-based stress reduction program. *Journal of Behavioral Medicine.* 2008; 31: 23–33.

Childre, D., and Marti, H. (1999). *The heartmath solution.* New York, NY: HarperCollins, 1999. www.HeartMath.com.

Davidson, R. J., Kabat-Zinn, J., Schumacher, J., et al. Alterations in brain and immune function produced by mindfulness meditation. *Psychosomatic Medicine.* 2003; 65: 564–570.

Davis, J. M., Fleming, M. F., Bonus, K. A., and Baker, T. B. A pilot study on mindfulness based stress reduction for smokers. *BMC Complementary and Alternative Medicine.* 2007; 7: 2. Retrieved November 8, 2012, from www.biomedcentral.com/1472-6882/7/2.

Dyer, W. (2002). *Getting in the gap: Making conscious contact with God through meditation.* Carlsbad, CA: Hay House, 2002.

Farb, N.A.S., Segal, Z. V., Mayberg, H., Bean, J., McKeon, D., Fatima, Z., and Anderson, A. K. Attending to the present: Mindfulness meditation reveals distinct neural modes of self-reference. *Social Cognitive and Affective Neuroscience.* 2007; 2(4): 313–322.

Fehmi, L. *Open Focus.* The Princeton Biofeedback Centre, LLC. Retrieved November 7, 2012, from www.openfocus.com/resources/complimentary-programs.

Fehmi, L. (2010). *Dissolving pain: Simple brain training exercises for overcoming pain.* Boston: Trumpeter Books.

Fehmi, L. (2007). *The open focus brain.* Boston: Trumpeter Books.

Feldman, G., Hayes, A., Kumar, S., Greeson, J., and Laurenceau, J. P. Mindfulness and emotion regulation: The development and initial validation of the Cognitive and Affective Mindfulness Scale-Revised (CAMS-R). *Journal of Psychopathology and Behavioral Assessment.* 2007; 29: 177–190.

Greeson, J., and Brantley, J. (2008). Mindfulness and anxiety disorders: Developing a wise relationship with the inner experience of fear. In: Didonna, F. (Ed.). *Clinical handbook of mindfulness.* New York, NY: Springer, pp. 171–188.

Grossman, P., Tiefenthaler-Gilmer, U., Raysz, A., and Kesper, U. Mindfulness training as an intervention for fibromyalgia: Evidence of postintervention and 3-year follow-up benefits in well-being. *Psychotherapy & Psychosomatics.* 2007; 76: 226–233.

Grossman, P., Niemann, L., Schmidt, S., and Walach, H. Mindfulness-based stress reduction and health benefits. A meta-analysis. *Journal of Psychosomatic Research.* 2004; 57: 35–43.

HeartMath. HeartMath. www.HeartMath.com.

Hebb, D. *The Organization of behavior.* (2009). Mahwah, NJ: Lawrence Erlbaum Associates, Inc.

Hölzel, B. K., Ott, U., Gard, T., et al. Investigation of mindfulness meditation practitioners with voxel-based morphometry. *Social Cognitive and Affective Neuroscience.* 2007a; 3: 55–61.

Hölzel, B. K., Ott, U., Hempel, H., et al. Differential engagement of anterior cingulate and adjacent medial frontal cortex in adept meditators and non-meditators. *Neuroscience Letters.* 2007b; 421: 16–21.

Hölzel, B., Carmody, J., Evans, K., Hoge, E., Duse, J., Morgan, L., Pitman, R., and Lazar, S. Stress reduction correlates with structural changes in the amygdala. *Social Cognitive Affective Neuroscience*. 2010; 5(1): 11–17.

Hutcherson, C. A., Seppala, E. M., and Gross, J.J. I don't know you but I like you: Loving kindness meditation increases positivity toward others; Paper presented at the 6th annual conference Integrating Mindfulness-Based Interventions into Medicine; Worcester, MA: *Health Care & Society*; 2008.

Jacobson, Edmund. "The Progressive Muscle Relaxation of Dr. Edmund Jacobson." *HypnoGenesis*. Retrieved November 8, 2012, from http:///www.hypnos.co.uk/hypnomag/jacobson.htm.

Jain, S., Shapiro, S. L., Swanick, S., Roesch, S. C., Mills, P. M., Bell, I., and Schwartz, G.E.R. A randomized controlled trial of mindfulness meditation versus relaxation training: Effects on distress, positive states of mind, rumination, and distraction. *Annals of Behavioral Medicine*. 2007; 33: 11–21.

Jha, A. P. (2005). *Garrison Institute report: Contemplation and education: Scientific research issues relevant to school-based contemplative programs: A supplement*. New York: Garrison Institute. Retrieved July 3, 2012. From www.garrisoninstitute.org/component/docman/doc_view/56-contemplative-techniques-in-k-12-education-a-mapping-report?Itemid=66.

Jha, A.P., Krompinger, J., and Baime, M. J. Mindfulness training modifies subsystems of attention. *Cognitive, Affective & Behavioral Neuroscience*. 2007; 7: 109–119.

Kabat-Zinn, J. "Mindfulness Based Stress Reduction Program." *Center for Mindfulness*. University of Massachusetts Center for Mindfulness. Retrieved from www.umassmed.edu/Content.aspx?id=41254&LinkIdentifier=id.

Kabat-Zinn, J., Lipworth, L., Burney, R., and Sellers, W. Four-year follow-up of a meditation–based program for the self-regulation of chronic pain: Treatment outcomes and compliance. *Clinical Journal of Pain*. 1986; 2(3): 159–173.

Kabat-Zinn, J. Mindfulness-based interventions in context: Past, present, and future. *Clinical Psychology: Science and Practice*. 2003; 10: 144–156.

Kabat-Zinn, J., Wheeler, E., Light, T., et al. Influence of a mindfulness meditation-based stress reduction intervention on rates of skin clearing in patients with moderate to severe psoriasis undergoing phototherapy (UVB) and photochemotherapy (PUVA). *Psychosomatic Medicine*. 1998; 60: 625–632.

Kabat-Zinn, J. (1990). *Full catastrophe living: Using the wisdom of your body and mind to face stress, pain, and illness*. New York, NY: Delacorte Press.

Kaplan, J. (2008). *Mindfulness of Emotions*. Retrieved October 9, 2010 from http://urbanmindfulness.org/storage/UM%20Mindfulness%20of%20Emotions.pdf.

Kristeller, J. L, Baer, R. A., Quillian-Wolever, R. (2006). Mindfulness-based approaches to eating disorders. In: *Mindfulness-based treatment approaches: A clinician's guide to evidence base and applications*. San Diego, CA: Academic Press, pp. 75–91.

Lau, M. A., Bishop, S. R., Segal, Z. V., et al. The Toronto Mindfulness Scale: Development and validation. *Journal of Clinical Psychology*. 2006; 62: 1445–1467.

Ludwig, D. S., and Kabat-Zinn, J. Mindfulness in medicine. *Journal of the American Medical Association*. 2008; 300: 1350–1352.

Lutz, A. S., Slagter, H. A., Dunne, J., and Davidson, R. J. Attention regulation and monitoring in meditation. *Trends in Cognitive Sciences*. 2008a; 12: 163–169.

Meditation Society of America, Meditation Station, *OM*. Retrieved November 8, 2012, from www.meditationsociety.com/week20.html.

Morone, N. E., Greco, C. M., and Weiner, D. K. Mindfulness meditation for the treatment of chronic low back pain in older adults: A randomized controlled pilot study. *Pain*. 2008; 134: 310–319.

Newberg, A. B., Wintering, N., Waldman, M. R., Amen, D., Khalsa, D. S., and Alavi, A. Cerebral blood flow differences between long-term meditators and non-meditators. *Conscious Cognition*. 2010; 19(4): 899–905.

Ramel, W., Goldin, P. R., Carmona, P. E., and McQuaid, J. R. The effects of mindfulness meditation training on cognitive processes and affect in patients with past depression. *Cognitive Therapy and Research*. 2004; 28: 433–455.

Rosenzweig, S., Reibel, D. K., Greeson, J. M., et al. Mindfulness-based stress reduction is associated with improved glycemic control in type 2 diabetes mellitus: A pilot study. *Alternative Therapies in Health and Medicine*. 2007; 13: 36–38.

Ruden R. (2011). *When the past is always present*. New York, NY: Routledge. www.Havening.org.

Ruden R. (2013). Personal communication. January 5, 2013.

Schonert-Reichl, K., and Lawlor, M. (2010). The Effects of a Mindfulness-Based Education Program on Pre- and Early Adolescents' Well-Being and Social and Emotional Competence. *Mindfulness*.   http://thehawnfoundation.org/wp-content/uploads/2012/12/KSR-MSL_Mindfulness_2010-copy.pdf.

Siegel, D. (2010). *Mindsight. The new science of personal transformation*. New York, NY: Bantam Books.

Smith, Steven. "Walking Meditation." *The Center for Contemplative Mind in Society*. Retrieved November 8, 2012, from www.contemplativemind.org/practices/tree/walking-meditation.

Tang, Y. Y., Ma, Y., Wang, J., et al. Short-term meditation training improves attention and self-regulation. *Proceedings of the National Academy of Sciences*. 2007; 104: 17152–17156.

The Dalai Lama. (2001). *An open heart: Practicing compassion in everyday life*. New York, NY: Little, Brown and Company.

Walach, H., Buchheld, N., Buttenmuller, V., Kleinknecht, N., and Schmidt, S. Measuring mindfulness—the Freiburg Mindfulness Inventory. *Personality and Individual Differences*. 2006; 40: 1543–1555.

Winbush, N. Y., Gross, C. R., and Kreitzer, M. J. The effects of mindfulness-based stress reduction on sleep disturbance: A systematic review. *Explore* (NY). 2007; 3: 585–591.

Zautra, A. J., Davis, M. C., Reich, J. W, et al. Comparison of cognitive behavioral and mindfulness meditation interventions on adaptation to rheumatoid arthritis for patients with and without history of recurrent depression. *Journal of Consulting and Clinical Psychology*. 2008; 76: 408–421.

Zylowska, L., Ackerman, D., Yang, M., et al. Mindfulness meditation training in adults and adolescents with ADHD: A feasibility study. *Journal of Attention Disorders*. 2008; 11: 737–746.

FURTHER READING

Berstein P. (2005). "Intuition: What Science Says (So Far)." Trans. Array. *Endophysics, Time, Quantum and the Subjective*. Rosolino Buccheri et al. (Eds.). Singapore: World Scientific Publishing.

Biegel, G., Brown, K., Shapiro, S., and Schubert, C. Mindfulness-based stress reduction for the treatment of adolescent psychiatric outpatients: A randomized clinical trial. *Journal of Consulting and Clinical Psychology*. 2009; 77: 855–866.

Britta, K., Hölzel, J., et al. Mindfulness practice leads to increases in regional brain gray matter density. *Psychiatry Research: Neuroimaging*. 2011; 191 (1): 36.

Flook, L., Smalley, S. L., and Kitil, M. Effects of mindful awareness practices on executive functions in elementary school children. *Journal of Applied School Psychology*. 2010; 26: 1, 70–95.

Hawn Foundation. (2011). *The MINDUP Curriculum, Grades Pre-K – 2*. New York, NY: Scholastic Inc.

Hooker, K., and Fodor, I. Teaching mindfulness to children. *Gestalt Review*. 2008; 12(1): 75–91.

Kaiser, Greenland S. (2010). *The mindful child*. New York, NY: Free Press.

Kaslow, N. J., and Racusin, G. R. (1994). Family therapy for depression in young people. In W. M. Reynolds & H. F. Johnston (Eds.), *Handbook of depression in children and adolescents: Issues in clinical child psychology*. New York, NY: Plenum Press, pp. 345–363.

Miller, A. L., Wyman, S. E., Huppert, J. D., et al. Analysis of behavioral skills utilized by suicidal adolescents receiving dialectical behavior therapy. *Cognitive and Behavioral Practice*. 2000; 7: 183–187.

Moustafa, B. M. (1999). Multisensory approaches and learning styles theory in the elementary school (Descriptive Report). Retrieved November 8, 2012, from www.eric.ed.gov/ERICWebPortal/search/detailmini.jsp?_nfpb=true&_&ERICExtSearch_SearchValue_0=ED 432388&ERICExtSearch_SearchType_0=no&accno=ED432388.

Ott, M. J. Mindfulness meditation in pediatric clinical practice. *Pediatric Nursing*. 2002; 28: 487–491.

Piaget, J. The stages of the intellectual development of the child. *Bulletin of the Menninger Clinic*. 1962; 26, 120–128.

Posner, M. I., and Petersen, S. E. The attention system of the human brain. *Annual Review of Neuroscience.* 1990; 13: 25–42.

Semple, R. J., Lee, J., Rosa, D., and Miller, L. A randomized trial of mindfulness-based cognitive therapy for children: Promoting mindful attention to enhance social-emotional resiliency in children. *Journal of Child and Family Studies.* 2010; 19: 218–229.

Semple, R. J., Lee, J., and Miller, L. F. (2006). Mindfulness-based cognitive therapy for children. In R. A. Baer (Ed.). *Mindfulness-based treatment approaches: Clinicians guide to evidence base and applications.* Oxford, UK: Elsevier, pp. 143–166.

Siegler, R. S. (1991). *Children's thinking* (2nd ed.). Upper Saddle River, NJ: Prentice-Hall.

Stahl, B., and Goldstein, E. (2010). *A mindfulness-based stress reduction workbook.* Oakland, CA: New Harbinger Publications, Inc.

Thompson, M., and Gauntlett-Gilbert, J. Mindfulness with children and adolescents: Effective clinical application. *Clinical Child Psychology and Psychiatry.* 2008; 13: 395.

Verduyn, C. (2000). Cognitive behavior therapy in childhood depression. *Child Psychology and Psychiatry Review.* 2000; 5: 176–180.

Wagner, E. E., Rathus, J. H., and Miller, A. L. (2006). Mindfulness in dialectical behavior therapy (DBT) for adolescents. In R. A. Baer (Ed.). *Mindfulness-based treatment approaches: Clinician's guide to evidence base and applications.* Oxford, UK: Elsevier, pp. 143–166.

Wall R. B. Tai chi and mindfulness-based stress reduction in a Boston public middle school. *Journal of Paediatric Health Care.* 2005; 19: 230–237.

Wallace, B. Alan. (2006). *The attention revolution: Unlocking the power of the focused mind.* Boston, MA: Wisdom Publications.

Wislock, R. F. What are perceptual modalities and how do they contribute to learning? *New Directions for Adult & Continuing Education.* 1993; 59: 5–13.

About the Author

Debra Burdick, LCSW, BCN, also known as "The Brain Lady," is a Licensed Clinical Social Worker and a board certified Neurofeedback practitioner. She is a national speaker and author and has been providing outpatient psychotherapy and mindfulness skills to her clients since 1990. She added neurofeedback to her psychotherapy practice in 1999. She is an expert author on SelfGrowth.com.

Debra specializes in ADHD, depression, anxiety, stress, sleep, cognitive function, relationships, mindfulness, and traumatic brain injury. Besides her private practice, Debra worked at the Child Guidance Clinic, Family Services, Child and Family Agency, and Lawrence and Memorial Hospital in New London, CT. She teaches all-day workshops including *A Holistic Approach to Success with ADHD* and *Mindfulness Toolkit: A Practical Experiential Workshop of Mindfulness Skills*. Mindfulness training for business leaders and executives is another of her passions.

Debra developed her own mindfulness practice to deal with a chronic illness (now thankfully healed). She found it so helpful in her own life that she started teaching her clients the skills she was using. She went on to develop clinical material on mindfulness skills and created a four-step process for working with clients using mindfulness that she perfected in her private practice and in an intensive outpatient program. Her clients have shown her that mindfulness skills improve the rate and quality of treatment outcomes.

Debra has extensive experience helping children and adults thrive with ADHD. In addition to counseling hundreds of clients over the past 20 years, she parented a daughter who has ADHD, was married to a man with ADHD, and was business partners with someone with ADHD. She combines knowledge gained from her own personal healing journey, her parenting experience, her clients, and her professional study of ADHD and brain dysregulation into her holistic approach.

Her books and CDs include:

- IS IT REALLY ADHD? ONLY ADHD? How to Get an Accurate Diagnosis for You or Your Child
- ADHD and Sleep—Children and Adults; Sleep Better Tonight
- ADHD Treatment Options. How to Choose the Right Treatment for You or Your Child
- A Holistic Approach to Successful Children with Attention Deficit/ Hyperactivity Disorder—A Home Study System for Parents
- Meditations for Concentration
- Mindfulness Toolkit CD

Debra continues to teach numerous presentations, workshops, and teleseminars. She is often interviewed on Internet radio and her work has been featured in *The Day* newspaper, *Self-Improvement* magazine, and Parenting Powers television show.

For more information visit www.TheBrainLady.com. Contact author at Deb@TheBrainLady.com.

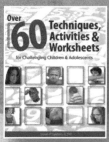

Made in the USA
San Bernardino, CA
09 May 2014